'Juno's writing is brilliantly personal and honest and always funny. Here, as usual in her work, the thought and theory are led by feeling and are so much more powerful for it. Her interviewees are among the most important trans and nonbinary people in the world today. *Trans Power* is not to be missed!'

— *Amelia Abraham, author of* Queer Intentions: A (Personal) Journey Through LGBTQ+ Culture

'In *Trans Power*, Juno Roche shows us the space we already have to be ourselves. Juno Roche's trans superpower is generosity – from the very first pages, I felt a deep sense of kinship, of being welcomed into an intimate conversation about what it can mean to be trans. *Trans Power* is a respite, a compendium of maps to the new place and a portal for seekers and makers of liberation.'

— *Andrea Lawlor, author of* Paul Takes the Form of a Mortal Girl

'*Trans Power* really captures the diversity of the trans experience – essential reading for people who want to gain a better understanding of trans people or for trans people trying to better understand themselves.'

— *Charlie Craggs, activist and author of* To My Trans Sisters

'An absolute gem. Juno weaves her own powerful words into the words of other inspirational trans people and the result is exactly the title: trans power.'

— *Fox Fisher, artist, filmmaker and trans campaigner*

'*Trans Power* certainly lives up to its name: an empowering, emboldening and ground-breaking book that will bolster generations to come. Absolutely brilliant.'

— *Owl, writer, filmmaker and trans campaigner*

by the same author

Queer Sex
A Trans and Non-Binary Guide to Intimacy,
Pleasure and Relationships
Juno Roche
ISBN 978 1 78592 406 4
eISBN 978 1 78450 770 1

of related interest

Life Isn't Binary
On Being Both, Beyond, and In-Between
Meg-John Barker and Alex Iantaffi
ISBN 978 1 78592 479 8
eISBN 978 1 78450 864 7

Transgressive
A Trans Woman on Gender, Feminism, and Politics
Rachel Anne Williams
ISBN 978 1 78592 647 1
eISBN 978 1 78592 648 8

Trans Love
An Anthology of Transgender and Non-Binary Voices
Edited by Freiya Benson
ISBN 978 1 78592 432 3
eISBN 978 1 78450 804 3

**Everything You Ever Wanted to Know about Trans
(But Were Afraid to Ask)**
Brynn Tannehill
ISBN 978 1 78592 826 0
eISBN 978 1 78450 956 9

Written on the Body
Letters from Trans and Non-Binary Survivors
of Sexual Assault and Domestic Violence
Edited by Lexie Bean
*Foreword and additional pieces by Dean Spade, Nyala Moon,
Alex Valdes, Sawyer DeVuyst and Ieshai Bailey*
ISBN 978 1 78592 797 3
eISBN 978 1 78450 803 6

To My Trans Sisters
Edited by Charlie Craggs
ISBN 978 1 78592 343 2
eISBN 978 1 78450 668 1

TRANS POWER

Own Your Gender

Juno Roche

Jessica Kingsley *Publishers*
London and Philadelphia

First published in 2020
by Jessica Kingsley Publishers
73 Collier Street
London N1 9BE, UK
and
400 Market Street, Suite 400
Philadelphia, PA 19106, USA

www.jkp.com

Library of Congress Cataloging in Publication Data
A CIP catalog record for this book is available from the Library of Congress

British Library Cataloguing in Publication Data
A CIP catalogue record for this book is available from the British Library

ISBN 978 1 78775 019 7
eISBN 978 1 78775 020 3

Printed and bound in Great Britain

Dear one-of-a-kind friend,

I dedicate this book to you with every ounce of love and tenderness in my being. I made it, Avalon, I got here. We both know I fucked up more often than most, but not with you, never with you. You taught me boundaries; you taught me how to respect myself and others. You were my sister, my brother, my dearest friend and my protector.

I'll carry our memories for as long as I'm here: the ranch in Nevada, the late-night trains back to Barcelona, smashed in Soho, partying in San Francisco and dancing in every 'one-nighter' that London threw up before us. So many beautiful, laughter-filled memories.

I miss you, Avalon.

Avalon Karen Cummings
6 April 1964–14 July 2018

We are all different from each other. This is how it is in the society we live in; though we all look alike, we are different from each other.

To respect each other is so important for humanity and equally so is to learn to love one another.

Always be brave & beautiful both inside and out.

Dr April Ashley MBE
London, September 2018

CONTENTS

TRANS-CENTRAL

'Help!' No really, 'Help!'

I know that opening this book with a cry for help might seem (it does seem) a little (a lot) needy, but I am having a huge crisis in confidence as I don't feel like a woman (or a man) anymore; nor do I feel nonbinary as it includes the word 'binary'; and nor do I feel fluid as it still posits two binary poles for me to become fluid between.

I feel trans.

And finally, I feel beautifully cut adrift from the endless layers of performativity that have weighed me down my whole life.

Layers of performativity: I'm sure they have blocked any dysphoria from leaving me and allowed it instead to remain deep inside, turning to self-stigma and ultimately internalised transphobia. We do that. How could we not when the world throws so much transphobic shade our way, constantly telling us that 'we are not good enough to be considered as real'? How could we not internalise that in our endless quest to become perfect binary specimens for them?

Those layers of performance were me trying to please everyone else in the world but me.

I have disconnected from those layers now because my label is simply 'trans' and I have no idea how to perform trans, or if I need to. On the one hand, that's terrifying; on the other, utterly freeing. All those layers of expectation which are thrust upon us – boy, masculine, femme-boy, femme, transgender, gender, passing, sexy, fuckable, sexual, woman, real – are such a weight to carry around. It's taken physically moving to the middle of nowhere in the Spanish mountains to start to rid myself of the performance-memory that clustered around my frontal lobe every time I went to leave the house; the cloak of performance that enabled me to feel good enough to walk down the street, even when I appeared to be good enough or people told me that I was good enough on their terms.

'Not to worry,' they said, 'no one would ever know. You look just like a woman.'

I've cut adrift from all that now, I'm simply trans, and I'm not sure trans needs dressing up in any particular way or style. How do you dress or perform a prefix?

I feel trans.

I feel trans and maybe queer.

My queerness and transness feel vast and open like the Serengeti Plain. Trans was always my destination. I can see it now – I see that's where I've always been heading. Not to woman or man – I hate being pinned down like that.

I feel transgressive. I feel hybrid.

But not first-stage hybrid like the early semi-electric cars that only went at 4 mph and only had the battery life of an aged alarm clock. No, I feel 'developed hybrid' or 'sophisticated hybrid', like a new species that has existed for a while yet has seldom been encountered so we don't have the words to describe them, to describe me. Like a hybrid that at one point in history was born of male and female expectations but now is something completely different.

Trans, just the prefix, no need for woman as in trans-woman or gender as in trans-gender. I like the thought that we as trans are a prefix to some change that is brilliantly underway but as yet unresolved and partially unrecognisable. People, feminists, biological essentialists and bigots are still arguing the logic of the smattering of stuff they think they know and accept, the gender constructs and constraints. They can't see that a party has truly started, off over there in a far corner, where fireworks are exploding, drowning out their pointless skirmish over the word 'real'. We are the prefix to change and we can see from this backlash and the emerging fundamental differences in the gendered landscape that change is afoot. The genie is way out of the bottle. They know deep down that we are winning and that so we should, as we are only adding to this world, not subtracting.

Deep down though, I sometimes wish I could avoid being trans and transgressive because it feels like a lonely path and, honestly, I'm a little bit tired of being on my own. I'm desperate for some shared sexual pleasure or intimate action – a kiss, oral sex, a bite on my nipple, a hug...anything – before I forget how to do skin on skin with another, before I forget what a kiss feels like.

I want intimate but light, airy dates. I'm in a place that feels brilliant but confusing and lonely. A space I can't run away from if I want to be kissed. I've got lips for kissing, I think?

I've got nothing left to give to the gender binary, even though I might get kissed in its shadow. Naming myself 'woman' allowed for easier kissing. Naming myself 'trans' seems to create a divide between me and the kissing world. Why?

But, I repeat, I have nothing more to give to the broken, defunct, damaging, limiting system of gender binaries. Nothing, not even a single breath. I'm all out of caring to even try to locate me within its parameters. I thought I would slip easily into 'trans woman' and perhaps just 'woman' but no, I've turned 180 degrees away to my new buddy, trans.

The gender binary I've realised is empty because it doesn't really exist – not as a real thing like a tree or the ground we walk on. It's just a construct we spend our lives chasing and failing at, an insidiously silent construct that pretends not to exist when challenged: 'Sexism, it's all in your head; it's banter.' It traps all of us and we have to work hard to get out from its grasp. I thought I needed permission to try to enter or leave it. I think it's a working-class thing to submit without question and stay – you are taught to be thankful. I spent years trying to find comfort, confidence and love within its bounds but to no avail. Stupidly I thought it would be home. I thought it might reward me for trying so hard to uphold its structures. I thought the binary was a two-way 'give and take' thing.

It's not like I'm naive and have lived under a comfortable moss-covered stone, or have sheltered in the wilds of the countryside or deep in academia. No. I've been an addict, a sex worker, a truck driver, a drug runner and an assistant head teacher.

I've been single, married, divorced (twice), monogamous and open. I've been kink, I've been vanilla – I've been to sex and Tupperware parties. I've tried relentlessly to find my place within the binary gender structure. But it's not happening. It's just not happening. I want to live my life freely and weightless outside of a performed frame. I want – no, I need – to own every millimetre of my trans body, I want trans-ecstasy. I want to be trans and to be free.

By the end of my last book, *Queer Sex*, I'd come to a conclusion that was troubling and deeply unexpected. I realised through the process of interviewing brilliant and inspiring people that I absolutely had to give away three words in order to start down the road to comfort and pleasure in my body.

The words 'real', 'woman' and 'vagina'.

Words I have spent the greater part of my life struggling to own, inhabit and use.

I struggled to hold onto the word 'woman' at the start of my transition as people all around me told me I'd be ugly and unconvincing and that no one would believe I was a woman. I fought for the word 'woman' when people were telling me I needed to get voice coaching, walking and sitting coaching, eating coaching (I kid you not), and that in order to be seen as a 'real' woman I'd need to get the whole of my face and parts of my body de-masculinised. Would I consider, for example, removing ribs, chin bones and having my Adam's apple shaved, even though people had always made fun of me for never having one. Kids at school said, 'You can't be a boy, you don't have an apple.' I daydreamed about having an Adam's apple removed that was never there. That's some kind of deep dysphoric shit.

I struggled to hold onto the word 'woman' as I lined up with every other trans person in the ever-increasing line for surgery. I struggled to inhabit the word 'woman' when the letters H, I and V seemed to take hold of everything in my life and placed gender realignment surgery way out of my reach. I struggled for the word 'woman' with my cock and balls between my legs, and then I struggled some more for the word 'woman' when the cock and balls had been refashioned into a thing they called a 'vagina', my sweet cave. I struggled for days after the surgery when the surgeon came round and pushed a speculum deep inside my newly created cavity, just so he could tell me my cunt-depth, my fuckability. That day, inside my head I shucked the word 'woman' as it quite literally meant 'no-power' in a patriarchal world; or to be more precise, this patriarchal ward.

I was advised by 'friends' in those very early days of my 'coming-into-being' not to transition as I'd be laughed at and that no one in the world would ever desire me as 'unconvincing woman'. I would be alone, they said, the HIV positive trans woman alone.

Those words of advice slipped insidiously under my skin and became some kind of self-stigmatising, unwitting truth. I believed I was beyond touch. I still have the trace of that legacy now, I'm ashamed to admit, despite U=U (undetectable equals untransmittable), despite an undetectable viral load, I still suffer from feeling that I am too much responsibility for anyone to bear. Too trans, too HIV. Look away, for fuck sake, look away.

But that negative advice, or the way it made me feel, isn't the reason why I have to give those words, 'woman', 'real' and 'vagina', away. Words that will leave me temporarily, or perhaps permanently, unable to simply explain myself or my body in this lifetime or this contemporary cultural frame(s) of reference. Those words for me and my body don't fit or feel appropriate anymore. I don't feel connected in any constructive way to the set gender binaries. I want to detach what little binary memory or actuality remains, not reattach it, through my transition, to the other side. I want only to be known as trans; not woman, not man. Woman or man, for me, muddies my transness. Femme or masculine muddies my transness.

Trans is empowerment and autonomy – inhabiting my frame and my frames of reference. It's being present in every part of me. There isn't a shred or sliver of regret about my convoluted journey. I adore being here in my life. I shouldn't have to say it but I will for those who, perhaps rightfully or demandingly, need to hear it:

'I have no regrets at all, not a single moment of regret.'

My cock and balls make complete sense, now inverted to create a cave: my cock head and shaft whittled down to form a kind of clitoral stand-in, a comedy clit [boom, boom]; sections of my scrotal sac stitched to my cock skin to form the cave (quite a shallow cave but deep enough nonetheless for sexual exploration).

I have no desire to achieve an acceptable 'binary-balance' for the world to be able to pigeon hole me as a 'trans woman who looks and acts woman enough to be allowed in'. The word 'woman' was unhelpful for me in almost every way going. It didn't land and contain me anymore than the word 'man' did.

I don't want an X on my passport – X marks the spot for what?

I want a **T**, a great fucking fat zinging **T**, with bells on and a fanfare.

A proud **T** that stands alone without qualification. A proud **T** that is built on a plethora of genitalia and different genital configuration models. A proud **T** presence is usually defined as an object of promiscuity, as if, as a body, it wants all options open. I do. I want to feel alive and promiscuous, like an installation artist who can utilise and use all of the materials in the world, not just the oil or acrylic paint. I want my body to have a plethora of options and routes. I'm not talking about being sexually promiscuous in this instance but rather promiscuous in the sense of losing the forced patterns of gender and becoming much more open and loose to my shifting feelings and emotions. Trans represents freedom to me, not just a place to stay put in a borrowed surface or on borrowed time.

I'm not lamenting the loss of male or female defining words or masculine or feminine terms; in fact, quite the opposite. I'm ecstatic about the words that work for me: 'trans' and 'queer'. Neither of them fall down on the side of femininity or masculinity, and neither of them have to adopt an oppositional position, an anti-position. I wish I could simply say 'I'm nonbinary' but I'm tired of being in direct opposition to something I don't even believe in.

If I am walking away from the binary, then I walk away from both sides towards my trans centre. It is a positive space, not oppositional. I'm no longer even sure if there is any purchase in my describing myself as 'trans-femme' or 'nonbinary femme', as it confuses me. Why would femme be any more pertinent than masculine if I am trying to reject such constructs as flimsy and judgemental?

I want to smash the patriarchy, not uphold or cherry pick parts of it. We can all play with the binaries to our hearts' content if it makes us happy, but we can do that without having to affix our value to one side or the other, by naming and renaming. Why do we allow the 'net worth' to still exist within binary spaces, when it's so reductive?

The endless naming and renaming is punishing and – in the context of trying to create greater freedom – pointless, as we are simply fighting to gain entry into the patriarchal structures that see us as 'other' and freaks. Sadly, but inevitably, the more we as trans folk chase 'pass' or 'blend' through feminisation or masculinisation, the more we add to the very structures of patriarchy that seek to destroy us. It is a vicious circle that exists tail to tail, and in our short lifetimes who can blame anyone for not wanting to step outside of it? But the truth is that unless we find other ways, apart from satisfying patriarchal norms, then we never challenge the accepted structures that patronise (you pass), ridicule (you're trying too hard) and violate (violence) us.

I moved away from male because it never felt real to me, I could never inhabit it as a performative layer. I tried to walk like a cowboy and merely became clumsy and fell over time and time again. The cost of falling and failing defined me as 'life-accidental'. I became a point of ridicule, the effeminate target-kid full of stitches with a father I could never please. People didn't call me a cowboy; they called me the sissy penguin kid with two left feet.

As I moved away from attempting to be male by using layers of learnt performativity (the cowboy, etc.), I presumed I was moving towards female. I did spend some real time there trying to make 'her' work, but I never felt woman, so I merely floated up and out of my skin like I did as a child whilst failing at being a boy.

I only really moved into my body when I arrived at the word 'trans'. 'Trans' alone, with no addition, base or stem. Trans is my label, my mate, my bedfellow and my confidante.

I now have the keys to my trans home and I've fucking taken up residency.

Finally I feel more beautiful than I ever have in all of my fifty-something years. I know at this age we're supposed to be lamenting the loss of youth, but I'm not. I'm revelling in the gloriousness of my queerness and transness. To be honest, it feels like I'm existing outside of age. I have learnt how to touch my body intimately, sexually and with great self-care. I respect my identity and I have even learnt to love, accept and stroke the downy hair around my arsehole. That's how far I have travelled since the end of the last book. I don't avoid any part of my body.

The word 'trans' is the one that fits me now like a glove. Like a beautiful soft, old leather glove. It feels like I have only ever been this word 'trans', even though for many years I didn't know it. Born trans, born this way.

Were my genitals ever really gendered or were they always simply trans-genitals with the capacity for change? Was my body always a trans body, never binary, never gendered? All those socialised and structural learnings around how to act to lessen the external attacks and condemnations. I was taught to not be natural but to act to please others via unnatural performance. Even throughout the process of transitioning, I have had to fight to please myself and not please those outside of me who deem me not good enough, too freakish or just not real (often other trans folk who see me as transgressive and troublesome).

I need to feel that the words I use for me and my body fully enclose and embrace all of my process, my struggle and the very core of my identity, the very nub of me.

Trans does.

I don't want to rely on the constant repetition or the constant renaming of 'I'm woman, woman, woman' and 'I'm real, real, real' to gain access to the greater – or at least the larger – gender binary framework. I don't feel 'found' or 'seen' there; in truth, looking back, I never have. I always felt like an outsider-outside, until 'trans' came along and allowed me the capacity of real feeling and touch.

I cannot find (fuck knows, I've really tried) my value within the word 'woman'. It just isn't happening, and now it's mine to own it still makes no difference. I find my meaning and my value – erotic, spiritual, conceptual, actual and economic – in the word 'trans'.

I honestly feel that my realignment surgery made me more trans, not more woman. Nothing new was added in the surgery: no additional skin, no cells, not a single blood cell. Everything used to fashion my cave was already there. In their new form my genitals simply allow me access to my inherent meaning. They allow me to go deeper than cunt-depth to my very essence.

The hormones I take every day make my trans exquisite and nuanced, not more feminine. They enable my body and my sense of self to be taken to new understandings, in a completely different direction: not to woman, not to man, but to an unknown place I haven't yet grown anywhere near accustomed to. On a daily basis my hormones reiterate my transness, our beautifully complex yet simple journey.

We trans folk were sold a pup that trans meant transition, or to 'pass through'. We were sold our label and its value as a place to avoid: close your eyes, hold your nose and pretty soon your transness will disappear in a puff of gender normativity. Our meaning was actually sold to us as further dysphoria.

I reclaim trans, even though trans alone is/was always ours;

it's just that we gave it away to please the rest of the world: 'Me trans? No, I'm just like you. I pass, don't I?'

My new sense of self allows me the strength and resilience to develop new ways of resisting the structures that have been so damaging in my life: patriarchy, sexism, classism and transphobia. And these things are not just supported by men – look at the current trans versus feminist struggle. Sexism and patriarchy are not upheld only by cis men and women. We trans folk are also often complicit in upholding those harsh standards. We could fight against the existing gender stereotypes but far too often we don't; we excuse ourselves as being 'new to the game' and 'learning' because we missed out in our teenage years. We capitulate far too readily to the commodity of binary gender and therefore patriarchy, and in doing so we condemn many of our siblings who cannot play the 'commodity-game'. This shit costs an awful lot.

My progress hasn't been linear. I've always felt open to mining my past and my wider history to make complete sense of my present. The dialectic between my cock and balls as they once were and as they are now, refashioned through surgery, is the space in which I continually discover my truth. I explore my body now as I would a work of art, its surface populated with divergent ideas that allow me to wander and dissolve into comfort to discover my meaning.

I don't want the straightjacket of control that the binary demands.

This transgressive, creative aim allows me to access and develop a language of understanding, intimacy and pleasure, a form of self-kindness that my life has been sorely lacking. To access kindness I had to accept and embrace the cock skin lining my cave.

I need my understanding of myself to start again from the ground up, without any feelings about what I should or shouldn't be, how I should or shouldn't act, or how I should or shouldn't present myself or my body. This isn't dress up or down.

I want to divest myself of all loaded meanings and find a new position in relation to patriarchy and the heteronormative constructs littering the gender binary. I find the words 'real woman' suffocating, as suffocating as I found the words 'real man'. In both cases I experienced society telling me I should inhabit one or the other, and how I should be doing that.

The words 'real woman' feel like a loop constructed from capitalism, patriarchy and recently stinging biological essentialism – cunt smells and dangerous cocks. A loop built hierarchically, with trans women at the bottom struggling to climb up a wet, muddy bank, desperate for purchase but constantly being kicked back down for not being 'real' enough. I can't engage with that thankless task anymore because, frankly, I don't want to fight to gain entry into that grubbily constructed zone. I disown that zone. I can do that as trans, I can fight patriarchy, misogyny and heteronormativity from the outside. I can still be a feminist and a socialist from out here.

Trans feels new, trans is literally buzzing. We should be jumping for joy at how we might create something decent and poetic in this hugely cynical and corrupt space. Trans is the change maker, trans is the prefix to future-all. I truly believe that we hold many of the answers that are currently needed.

I'm not talking about the 1950s model of trans as being an uber-woman or uber-man, built from a constant repetitive naming, renaming and citing of our evidence; real woman: lipstick, plucked eyebrows, long hair, soft skin. I feel I have little in common with those in the community seeking to be absorbed into those structures that already exist. I understand why and utterly respect their choices. I've tried to fit into those same evidencing structures, but it's not me. In the 50s, trans folk had very little choice about performativity – it was safety, it was life – but I have a choice (and actually feel I owe it to them), to work harder to challenge the existing structures that damage so many of us.

I feel adrift when I see and hear the trans community and our allies around me demanding, rightfully for them, that trans women are women and trans men are men. Completely legit.

Simple and completely legit, although I don't see many of our allies fucking us or being fucked by us. They are arms-distance allies, 'allies without intimacy', almost the opposite of 'friends with benefits'.

But I can see for the people saying that trans women are women and trans men are men, that it's true. They are men and women – simple, no debate. They don't need or want the trans prefix and they know exactly what they want to call their whole body and individual parts of their bodies. They assume a normative binary position because it works for them. I imagine it feels nice. Certainly, many trans folk do it brilliantly because it is their truth, constructed or not, and they are no different to our cis-siblings. Trans people never get the kudos they deserve for their brilliant transformations into the binary. It isn't easy. I'd always assumed that I'd be just like them and that normativity and acceptance were my bedfellows and endgame, but it's not for me. Being accepted within gender binary terms makes me feel more uncomfortable than residing outside of them. I'm not trying to rebel; I'm just finally being me and being present in my own lifetime.

In the opening page of *Queer Sex* I said that I questioned 'my ability to feel desirable and to view myself as a sexual being'. I realised after writing the book, when I slipped into a surprisingly bleak depressive indent, that I wasn't depressed because the world around me was saying that we as trans people are inauthentic. I was depressed because I realised that I still had work to do – masses of it. I couldn't see myself as sexual and desirable simply as a person subsumed into society's idea of womanhood. I didn't feel sexual or desirable, because I didn't feel like I was a woman. I was so tired of trying to be good enough for others, as woman or man. I was drained. But simply as trans I'm starting to feel like a completely fuckable fox who just isn't fucking yet.

In my depression, I knew that I had to work to do to repair the societal, historical dysphoria-damage. I'm still doing that, trying to make sense of this thing we encounter called 'dysphoria' whilst I reject the very labels that apparently solve any gender dilemmas. Isn't that the binary claim? Isn't that the claim, in our trans community/communities, that seeking to blend, to fit in and to pass as simply male or female will resolve the dysphoria? History is full of cis folk trying to please and blend into the gender binary to no avail. It's not like we are the sole owners of dysphoria; that shit exists all around, in every crack and crevice.

Aiming for a binary seat at the table may seem the most logical way to address dysphoria, but it doesn't even attempt to transgress or claim new, safe, unsullied ground; it merely adds our trans voices to a system that is inherently broken and ruthlessly corrupt. We get lost. We have words for that: 'blend', 'pass'. I would do that if it was in me, but it's not. This isn't academic;

I'm not trying to live out my life beyond the Butler-esque or the Bornstein.

This transgression is my easy.

We have a single life, that's my belief, so to live in transgression might appear tough. But I would put forward the idea that even when we seek out the comfort and safety of normativity and binary gender, we as trans folk still have to fight every day. Even those among us who do 'normal' supremely well, with great dignity and beauty, are continually fighting for tiny slivers of space, often through hails of abuse. We still have to rename ourselves constantly to be allowed in; and then once inside, we continue to have to evidence our naming until there is a quietness.

There seldom is quietness; someone always pipes up, 'Prove it.'

It is the space in which many trans folk lose their lives, the space where we try decently and respectfully to fit in. We are never encountered as 'gender-simple', as by definition we smash the binary and will always be seen outside of its structures. We hold an awful lot of the answers here to the whole shit show that is gender. We just have to believe it. Trans folk have to develop an inner confidence that allows us to become or own our radical.

After writing *Queer Sex* I knew that I had to step up to my own truth and reject the offer of binary acceptance that had always been put forward as the only option. I had to opt for my truth, which is actually much more straightforward but seems incredibly complex when set in a world that runs on the chugging, grubby steam of binary gender expectations. My truth, to be honest, also depresses me a little because I want to fuck, not be out campaigning on a new trans manifesto. I really want to be loved and hugged in this lifetime and not just be thanked for bold words (although the thanks are lovely, so thanks and here are some more bold words!).

I should have been full of joy after *Queer Sex*, but it was clear to me – even if I didn't say it aloud – that the book was my life/ is my life. I wrote it in real time as my emotions swirled up and spiralled down. It is a taut emotional journey that is only just starting.

The fact that it wasn't just a book to me but a personal journey was scary and depressing. I thought I was simply writing a book. Not to denigrate books, but I didn't realise that my life would be there on every page, in the words, the spaces, the questions I asked and the answers I listened to. I didn't notice the ways in which it changed me, day by day.

My life was there on the pages, getting increasingly tangled. I said in the last chapter that the book was a 'cry for help'. I remember writing the line and not knowing who I was crying to.

I do now – it was me. A cry inwards to let go and embrace the air in front of me that contained nothingness, a space to be filled with newness and transness. A space I didn't yet understand. No one had ever told me I could just be trans, that trans could be my destination. It was so overwhelming that in true Juno, fucked-up fashion I lay down to meditate, chant and do some yoga, and ended up wanking. Really wanking.

Perhaps wanking seemed like a better place to start than chanting. It was wanking, after all (the wondrous 'self-pleasure group'), that ended *Queer Sex*. I like the word 'wank' much more than 'masturbate' or 'self-pleasure'. It seems simple, honest and direct. Wanking is like eating, is like smoking – it occupies the hands and leaves the mind free to wander in and out of fantasies and sensations. The terms 'wanking' and 'jerking/

jacking off' are ones I want to reclaim from the historical, sexist division of language. Men are presumed to be the only ones who want to have quick, uncomplicated self-pleasure, while women are deemed to want something deeper and perhaps more mindful. Thus, the descriptors for women/feminine are 'self-pleasure' and 'masturbate', and for men/masculine they are 'wank' and 'jerk/jack off'. This posits a level of complexity and gravity to one and simplicity and immediacy to the other. I've been in both camps and neither is helpful. It also semi-excuses the difficulty that some trans folk find post-surgery or even post-hormones (femme) in accessing quick and easy pleasure, and puts the difficulty down to presumed inherent differences in gender pleasure. I want body response, not mental agility.

I find the term 'self-pleasure', ironically, to be a little bit 'wanky', and the term 'masturbate' to be too clinical. I find the words 'wanking' or 'wank' to be just about good enough to describe both the mechanics of what might happen and also the need to at least aim for an orgasmic point. So 'wanking' it is.

I needed a break from the swirling mass of noise in my mind that kept repeating: 'Your cock and balls are still there, just transformed into a new configuration. What are you going to call them?' Yoga and attempts at meditation just seemed to increase the noise. Accepting and embracing my old cock-and-ball skin was fundamental to my acceptance of me as a proud trans human being. But I had no words for what emerged from surgery. I still don't. I like 'cave' or 'orifice', but neither is perfect. But the struggle to find names allowed me to explore and to understand them by touch, smell and sensation.

I lay down and started to wank; and like the woman in the

book who went to bed every day for a year, I aimed to wank every day, or at least every other day until I became an expert in my own pleasure. I aimed to document this but I didn't, I'm sorry but I just enjoyed learning to wank again with my new configuration. My very own quest, complete with a magical old olive tree and a tiny chocolate-box house in the middle of the mountains. If only the neighbours knew what I was doing or could hear my moans... Wait, there are no neighbours! I still have no words but I do have a sense of how I feel pleasure.

My very first forays into wanking (post-*Queer Sex*) were occasional attempts at something that felt relatively normative and even (I'm embarrassed to say) traditional or conservative. Sometimes I would, as Michelle had suggested in *Queer Sex*, replace my once-a-week dilation with a wanking session. It went as follows:

Lay back on bed, moan a little and seductively open legs as in bad porn film, take vibrator in hand, and lube up with Liquid Silk (it has to be Liquid Silk), close eyes and whilst lubricating cave turn pink fleshy vibrator on to its lowest setting and rub across from nipple to nipple and back again.

Make nipples erect and with other hand pinch nipples hard to get to the pleasure/pain point.

My nipples have always been my erotic place especially in kink games. I love a clamp or a drip of hot wax. Hormones gave me huge nipples and so sensitive are they that sometimes even brushing them lightly turns me on.

Spend time playing with nipples, teasing them with the tip of the vibrator and pinching them with fingers. Close eyes and wait for ripples of pleasure to roll down to upcycled cock and ball area and wait. Occasionally look in mirror at face, nipples and crotch. Avoid lingering on eye bags.

Nothing below my belly button, nothing at all, my pleasure extending downwards into my ravine.

Persist waiting and then start again from nipple downwards.

Sometimes in my early post-*Queer Sex* wank days I'd watch very vanilla cis 'fuck porn', the kind of porn I literally have no sexual investment in as I don't want a cis man to fuck me. But for years I assumed this was going to be me – fucked hard by big cis dicks. So in my early exploration of wanking I watched vanilla cis porn. I would get distracted by the dialogue or the film set – I'm terrible with cheap bedding, and I'd critique clunky lines and dime-store furniture rather than his cock or her pussy – so I stopped watching cis porn.

Back to early wanking action:

Whilst pulling nipple and watching cis man fuck and say, 'Tell me it's the biggest', move vibrator down over belly, across my glorious 1980s bush, and place vibrator on cave entrance, then slowly push inside.

And wait. Nothing. Even with the purr of my vibrator pressed deep inside, nothing. I could write a shopping list, that's how little I felt: tinned tomatoes, celery, mushrooms…

All very Mills and Boon, a cock inside me and I make a shopping list.

There was something incredibly heteronormative about the way I imagined that I would plunge the vibrator deep inside and come whilst arching my back like a languid kitten. Despite knowing that I couldn't naturally lubricate, I still imagined that when I came I would somehow spurt fluid. I was still existing in my pre-trans structures of imagining 'what this would be like' rather than actually inhabiting my body and seeking new sensations.

My cock and balls are entirely different now: upcycled, refashioned and reconfigured. The space isn't imaginary, it's really there. I never read it as the vagina that I'd imagined for years I would, so I struggled at first to inhabit an imaginary place. I needed to locate myself and my pleasure within it. Transphobia had told me for years that the 'actual me' would never be good enough; even post-surgery we're deemed to be fake. I felt I should and would live in a performative layer of hyper-femininity and thus patriarchy. I maybe even imagined that I'd be okay with that.

To actually inhabit my upcycled cock and balls felt like an act of defiance and a cultural stance against all forms of attack – misogyny, sexism and the more recent feminist essentialist transphobia. I needed to occupy my very transness in order to discover my pleasure and to get away from the toxicity of arguments that swirl around and always reduce us to being 'just like them'.

Years of painful normativity have shaped me, and my body holds memories of those years. I realised that if my sweet cave held memories they would be painful, sad ones from the cock and balls I had rejected years earlier. Vaginoplasty did not come with new memories. It didn't add a new narrative. How could it?

I firmly believe that our bodies hold memories, imprints of memories, actions and reactions – on a cellular level we remember pleasure, pain and shame and respond accordingly, pulling away, recoiling or just letting go.

As an eight-year-old, I sat down on the toilet seat and took my mum's deep salmon, almost coral lipstick and coloured-in my cock and balls, trying to make them disappear.

They looked like prawns in a cocktail glass, a 1970s starter. I rejected them that many years ago, way back in the 1970s. Over thirty years of rejection and being ignored. 'Don't touch me there', I'd tell everyone I was intimate with, unless they were paying (I was on drugs, so cut me some slack). I have those memories deep in my dermis.

The collection of memories which lay latent in the space between my legs consisted of different layers: the rejection of maleness, the ingested shame that I wasn't femme enough to be seen as a woman and, more recently, the overlaid rejection of heteronormativity, gender normativity and female naming.

A sad bleak space. Soulless dead eyes peer into my cave. It was an unloved and misunderstood space.

To self-care and to wank, I had to own and love each and every layer and its memory. My sense of self, my transness, could only become powerful if I became 'one' with my whole history and bodily truth; if I rejected a neoliberal model of transness existing just as a surface, in favour of a model with a far grittier and complex truth.

The cock and ball combo that I spent years rejecting now lines a space they call a 'vagina' or 'neo-vagina'. I don't have a decent word for it yet, so I say 'cave'. It's not perfect – far from it – but it's not a 'vagina' or a 'neo-vagina'; those words don't respect my history or my body's history.

All in all, it's an utterly brilliant queer and trans space.

An apparently femme space, crafted from an apparently masculine totemic symbol, the 'cock'. The perfect male/female symbiosis, exquisitely fashioned and new.

Trans-genitals are awesome and should be encountered with utter respect and reverence.

Trans-genitals are both changed and change-makers.

Trans-genitals need documenting in words, watercolour and tapestry.

I continued to wank, experimenting with wanking, and then experimented some more, leaving the shores of what I thought I should do to arrive at the place where I just 'did' and 'felt'.

You get the picture.

I rediscovered my body not with another but with myself. I can be alone, just me, myself and my transness. It feels nourishing and lined with self-care. My transness is a joyful skin I'm in.

In wanking I have rediscovered the sweet spot in my arse, a space I'd stupidly and studiously avoided because I had put 'vagina' on a pedestal and decided that my 'pedestal-vagina' would be kink free – lusciously and virginally vanilla.

Push, pull, vanilla, virgin, vagina and missionary fuck.

My mind said, 'Use your hard-earned, hard-won vagina; vagina, vagina, vagina, inhabit only her, imagine a cock pushing in and you moaning, "Fuck me".'

My arse replied, 'No, fuck me! I'm the one you need with my easy-breezy pleasure and my ridiculously sweet "P-Spot". Go deeper, deeper, deeper, deeper. You know how this feels. Why ignore these feelings of pleasure?'

My mind rested for a week or two on my history and my love of kink, and then I let go, I just let go of the self-imposed hierarchy and shame that made me see 'vanilla-vaginal' entry at the top of the pyramid. 'Fuck that', I thought, as I studied my sweet arsehole and my competing femme cave in the mirror, feet planted high up. I love having two options. I realised that I didn't need to give one any more love or attention than the other. That was patriarchy and fantasy ruling my pleasure. That was 'I've waited years for a vagina to rescue me. Must use vagina only.' Bullshit.

I needed to do what felt pleasurable for me. I needed to feel it and not imagine it.

It was tough after surgery because there was a real sense that a vagina (neo) would be all the answers I ever needed to feel congruent. I had to let go of that and let go of the notion that in some way I was a virgin discovering sex for the first time. Sadly I realised that I was still somehow in the surgeon's hands whilst he was creating a 'brand, spanking-new vagina'. I knew sex, I knew my body. I just had to rediscover where the parts were and reacquaint myself with pleasure.

I discovered with the vibrator, and sometimes just with my fingers, that probing my arse deep inside and at the same time exploring around my front cave with the other hand, and across the tip of the remains of my cock, was heavenly. Using both holes for pleasure really works, and understanding the erectile tissue left behind between cock-tip-clit and cave enabled me to visualise what is there and what it is made out of. I could work with an old cock structure and understand that massaging the erectile tissue could and would and does lead to orgasm. Really great proper orgasms. Ironically, the female-looking bits hold very little pleasure, but relocating the cock bits and working with them and my prostate, does.

My new genitals are magical but they weren't created by

magic. I can play with the structures, the erectile tissue is hugely sensitive, I understand it, I can work with it. I finally understood that in trying to solely occupy the words 'real', 'woman' and 'vagina' I was still outside of my body, residing in the space which is defined by being 'just like the real thing'. It is a fantasy space, constructed from a construction, a perfect glimmering example of simulacra. I was endlessly waiting at the entrance to my vaginoplasty for pleasure and ignoring every other part of me. The parts that breathed, that moved, that smelt, that remembered and that were easy. At one point I thought they'd have to remove the excess erectile tissue but now I love it – it's so sensitive and unexpected. It sits in the space between the remains of what was my cock head and my cave opening, a ridge that becomes rock hard if I'm excited. It makes it quite difficult to penetrate my cave as it blocks the entrance, but nothing is increased or bettered, intensity or pleasure, by simple penetration. But exploring it gently, whilst fucking my arse, I feel masses of sensation, and emotionally I feel a kind, loving power-play between my two orifices. I love the interplay between the erectile tissue and my cave opening. Too aroused and it snaps shut so – like a game of cat and mouse – I have to listen and feel.

My arse really matters to my sexual pleasure; my prostate really matters. I know it can be found through the created vagina, but I haven't had much luck, I was never much good at following maps, preferring to stick to the routes I know. I'm planning to buy a prostate stimulator aimed at (gay) men, which is designed to stimulate the prostate through the arse. My old dysphoric shame would never have let me look at gay male sex toys post-surgery as I presumed I would be simply 'woman'. Like many trans folk, I avoided those give-away thoughts or conversations centred around still having a prostate. I briefly enjoyed the sense that all maleness was gone, but in the long term that just becomes a different kind of dysphoria.

Letting go of words allowed me to reconnect with my flesh, and that physical moment of pleasure was so far away from any gender construct I had ever experienced or suffered. No performed layers, just organs, flesh and sensitivity. Letting go of words, concepts and structures around those words allows me to explore my own sense of self and my own body by touch. It allows my fingers to access my truth and not my presumed desired outcome (i.e. a perfect, normative pussy).

If I am a performance it is a barely flickering one between male and female constructs, which vibrates continuously until both binaries become pointless and invisible. I cannot see any sense in them and I cannot find any reason to camp down in either place. I am at my happiest now, understanding myself and my body by touch, movement and physical response. It is never a name, merely an action, a movement, a reaction, a touch, sensation. When I first had surgery, there was an acceptance that you had to dilate 'through the pain' to keep your depth. Keeping depth was literally a physical construct to hold onto, but also a conceptual construct as the depth would define the space as a fully functional fuckable vagina. On the other hand, not dilating through the pain and accepting a shallower orifice as a logical outcome of using cock and ball skin is an acceptance of my skin and flesh, and the capacity of both to be pushed to a kind and comfortable place.

I stopped dilating beyond my threshold and allowed my body to rest in its new shape and contours.

I wank quite a lot now – not every day, but almost – often

outside in my courtyard, underneath my old olive tree. I feel sexual, and finally I'm starting to feel desirable. I'm just not sure yet who would be into me or who would be my sexual fit. Who is it I want to fuck with or be fucked by? I think I want to be fucked; arse-fucked though, not through a fantasy vaginal prism.

Maybe I want to be the one fucking?

Whilst wanking, I've started to visualise my genitals as being a mix or blend of both male and female, which they are. Female intent and male material. I spent years rejecting anything male or masculine on my body – hair, cock, balls, muscles, square lines, my voice and even the downy hair around my arsehole. Bless my poor arsehole!

All of those masculine triggers made it impossible to have a relationship with my body. I never felt like a boy or a man, so I rejected all of those physical aspects that were created in the slipstream of testosterone. I hated puberty because it simply embedded and increased the structural norms of masculinity: jaw, chin, cock, balls, hair, etc. But, realistically, my body is relatively unchanged now. Yes, hormones have made subtle differences (like really big plump nipples and a softening of muscles), and gender realignment surgery made a huge physiological and psychological difference. But that's it; everything else is still the same. My arms, my legs, my face, my chin, my arse, my feet and even the parts of my cock and balls that remain are the same – just reshaped to fit me and my sense of self. My cave is lined with cock and ball skin. In fact, there is no cave without the old cock skin; no cunt without the cock.

To be able to successfully wank I felt that I couldn't ignore, avoid, feel unattractive, or feel shame because my body is shaped mainly male/masculine. I couldn't avoid the inherent truth of my body, and I didn't want to anymore.

Avoiding vast parts of my body reduced me to only feeling desirable in the surgically created space between my legs and my hormone-induced big nipples, still surrounded by rings of sprouting hairs. I gave up trying to get rid of the hairs. I wanted to explore all of me and I wanted to feel whole, total, one surface. I didn't want to have to think about hair removal – plucking or waxing – every time I ran a hand across my surface. I didn't want to feel the discomfort of trying to shrink down my size 16/18 shoulders to a size I deemed as sexual in society's gaze.

So, and I know this sounds silly, I reclaimed all the masculine parts of me that I had rejected throughout my life as being unwanted and ugly. I thanked my cock and balls for helping to create a space that I can now explore with my legs open, lying on my back.

I literally, out loud, thanked my cock for always being there, even through the years of rejection. No one could have blamed it for upping and moving on to a new location where they could see the light of day. I conducted a 'one trans person ceremony' under my tree in which I reconnected with all of my body, every last inch. After the ceremony I ate figs and feta, just because I'm worth it.

I love my cock and balls now more than I ever have, even though if I took my knickers off [I'm single and happy so just ask], you would only see a reasonably convincing vagina. Quite a beautiful space. I feel a little sad that in *Queer Sex* I referred to it as an unwanted puppy that never gets walked.

I love puppies. I'm sorry [looks down and strokes puppy], I've moved on now.

I adore my cave. It's pink, tight and quite the little fighter, feisty when I want to enter her. The space needs gently and kindly cajoling. There is a fragility there because of the seams (the joins), and I also have to play a game with the erectile tissue because if it's too turned on and hard, the entrance becomes impassable.

Under my tree I've learnt to wank.

Credit where credit's due: How fucking cool are my cock and balls!

But they don't want any credit, awards or medals for their work. They allowed self-sacrifice in order for me to feel more at peace with my body and my shape – such a perfect feminist alliance.

It's a film waiting to happen.

But this isn't some academic, abstract or creative trade-off. My sex life isn't simply an exploration into trans feminism, or an exercise in semantics. I want to come, to have orgasms. I don't want people to find me clever or smart or risqué. I want to fuck and be fucked. I might owe at least part of my emerging world to both Bornstein and Butler – my inspiring double B's – but day to day I simply want to be intimate within my own trans body, by being present and by honouring my transness.

It matters that we talk about what our vaginas and cocks are made from because that's the great elephant in the room. Our femme-caves (I'll use that for accessible shorthand) are cut from cock and ball cloth. There is a sense in cis men that to fancy us is akin to being gay; that somehow our femininity and womanhood ends where our cocks line our sex caves; that somehow if a cis cock enters us, then it will be touching and caressing cock-skin legacy.

Enveloped in cock and ball skin. And it will be.

So, is your cock complaining? No. Get over yourself then.

Let's really talk about our bodies. Let's own our genitals proudly so that we aren't tense at the point of entry. Let's not simply hope for pussy-real-enough, pussy-pass-enough, pussy-perfect-enough. And it's not just trans femme spaces; trans cocks can be beautifully crafted from arm or leg skin and can have devices to pump them up into erections. How fucking sexy is that? What level of masculinity does it take to drive through that need for authenticity, to feel the attachment of a cock? I, for one, want to be fucked by that cock. I salute trans cocks in all their shapes, dimensions, materiality and dammed sexiness.

This reclaiming and renaming matter hugely to me. I know that language can feel, and far too often does feel, academic and privileged, full of class and posturing. But this isn't that; this is much more fundamental and actual.

If we constantly reject and demonise our bodies as not being good enough, then when we have changes made (say vaginoplasty, phallosplasty or breast augmentation), we still won't necessarily feel that we are good enough, because we have no intimate relationship with our bodies. We all see the endless photographs on Instagram seeking approval and seeking to be gaze-fucked, especially when all around society defines us as inauthentic and not good enough. I often wonder how many of our allies, however wonderful, would ever fuck or be fucked by us?

We can't simply keep adding to patriarchy without seeing the structural action of it chewing us up and spitting us out at exactly the same moment. We can afford to reach towards something more radical than absorption. When we keep knocking on the teasingly ajar door of patriarchy, we evacuate our space and our potential glory days; we become subsumed into the very structures which need our critique.

This isn't an academic 'Juno lies under the tree and seeks out a philosophical artsy standpoint for her cunt'. No, this is no Derridean-deconstructive meandering. This is real shit – maybe just for me (who knows?) but I doubt it. It makes perfect sense that if we spend years in a body that we reject, then the act of rejection itself won't allow us to develop a kind, loving relationship with our very skin, blood or bone. We reject our flesh and then imagine that surgical intervention will allow a nuanced complex relationship to develop naturally, and the rift between mind and body to be healed.

As I reclaim the elements of my cock and balls, I do so lovingly. I am finally present in my body.

I'm here, World, alive, wanking and ready under the big olive tree.

But with this new and deeper understanding of myself, it seems that there is still a price to be paid for rejecting normativity and the binary structures: I'm alone.

My internal and external clocks are ticking my life away, yet I'm still finding out about myself. I don't want to panic about time but I want to try to experience intimacy with another person, hopefully a trans person [shout out].

My lack of words for myself, especially my lack of acceptable labels, has got in the way of intimacy and fucking; 'Trans alone' is my label, but if I go onto a trans dating site I find reams of gender stereotypes which genuinely deep down do nothing for me. Nada.

Words like 'girly', 'smooth', 'soft', 'daddy', 'dominant seeks TS sub', 'sissy seeks top'. The list of words goes on and on and all they do is make me turn away and write angry words about smashing patriarchy. I'm not smooth, I'm not a sissy, I'm not looking for a father-figure or someone who wants to act out misogynistic fantasies. I want an equal.

I've rewritten my dating profile to look a little like this:

Transgender person who used to view their neo-vaginal space as a puppy but now sees that there is real magic going on down there: surgical, philosophical and cultural magic. Please, if you want to ask if I have had the operation, don't, because inevitably I am not the peep for you. It may be that I want to finger or fuck your arse as much as you want to explore my transness. My body is a temple to change and it documents me, society and feminism. I have scars. They are my history upon which your tongue might travel. They mark the passing of time from cock to cunt. If you can 'step up', do. If you can't, then thank you for existing in this space in which we are all looking for love and pleasure.

In joy, Juno.

P.S. I'd rather you be trans. Sorry if that sounds cis-phobic, but trans folk are my peeps x

Thank you, to the wondrous Kuchenga for imbuing me with the confidence to speak my truth online. Writing this profile made me feel like I was succeeding as a human. Kuchenga is one of the most alive human beings I have ever met.

But keeping it real here, my dating profile has received zero replies. Tell a lie, there was one: a man who said he'd read a piece by me in which I'd said that I used to be a 'prostitute' (his word not mine) and that I must be kidding myself if I thought I could earn money on this site at my age.

Cheek! I was looking for a kiss, not a paycheck!

I thought *Queer Sex* would at the very least lead me to kissing, but it didn't as I'm not ready yet... In my mid-fifties I'm still not ready. It's just me under the tree wanking and pondering. Just me, my fingers, a range of vibrators, occasionally some enlightened trans porn, sometimes the sun, always a yoga mat, my eyes closed and my fantasies.

I'm still in the solo game.

I'm where I need to be. And even though I only arrived here at one minute to fifty-five, I can't be scared of that. I still have work and exploration to do. For once in my life I'm going to get this right.

I need to say something, to be honest, even though on every level I hate myself for being weak enough to say it: I feel lonely. Simple. Just. Lonely. I have words and understanding but no kisses.

My life has gone at its own pace. I couldn't change that or rush my learning. I want this trans-embodied part of my life to be honourable and meaningful. I've been fucked before for a few quid. I can hold out now. I believe I'm worth it.

I want to share some of my remaining life with someone who really fits with me and I with them. Someone trans. They have to be trans. I love my trans family.

I refuse to give in to the fear that I have understood myself too late in the game. I believe it will still happen, even though I still haven't been kissed for years, like properly breath-stealing, heart-racing kissed. The kind of kiss that stops your world rigid still on a penny, as entwined lips slurp and exchange the intimacy of saliva. That kind of kiss.

I just need to be confident enough or open enough to allow that kiss to happen. I just have to be fully present in order to let that happen. I want to explore this space with other trans folk and people rejecting normative labels, people defining themselves as being gender nonconforming and people who push ever so gently at the edges; they're often where the real change takes place. In houses up and down the country *there are* brave, brilliant trans folk determined to make this a better space and to do that whilst having relationships, sex, intimacy and rich lives brimming with love and often self-confidence and success.

I need my community's help once again to help me understand how to be trans and intimate with the world. I get me now, but I just don't quite get how to move around the world as me and perhaps with another. I want to be trans and kissed. My head is full of questions about cocks made from arms and cunts made from cocks, about trans men being fucked in vaginas they proudly own and about trans women who love to fuck with an off-the-shelf cock. About what it means to be truly gender nonconforming and loved, and to find that love in a largely patriarchal space that deems trans to be a service station on the way to one binary town or another.

Selfishly, I miss the intimacy that built up during the process of interviewing people for *Queer Sex*. Up close and personal the trans community is a space of utter brilliance (and I mean brilliance in the sense of bright glimmering light). It can be overwhelming to be up close enough to feel the heart of our community beat. We are beacons of wonder.

This time I'm travelling far and wide to interview people I

find sexy, brave and charismatic – people you may know and people you may not know. But each in their own way they are forging new slivers of space. For some it's vast tracts of space, while others are content to make their domestic lives reflect their true selves.

I'm at that point just before the interviews start, and I'm alive with the excitement.

For all those beautiful people who have written to me on Twitter, Instagram, Facebook, via reviews or email, or who have simply come up to me in person, often offering hugs and congratulatory words that I never imagined *Queer Sex* could generate, this book is for you. Dive in, let's get serious and let's get a little bit dirty x.

TRAVIS ALABANZA

I recently lost a friend to cancer... A great friend, a friend I loved deeply, a really old friend I first met back in the late 1980s who lived in this part of London – the part I'm walking through to interview the wonderfully inspiring Travis Alabanza – the borders of Hackney and Stoke Newington. Travis is here to rehearse their new show 'Burgerz', based on an incident that happened around Travis as they walked over Waterloo Bridge. In an act of transphobia a passerby insulted Travis and then threw a burger at them. Travis talks about the people who witnessed the incident but carried on walking. The so-called innocent bystanders.

Travis is one of the most important creative voices in the trans and queer community: a poet, an artist and a performer. Travis's work is in great demand globally, and rightly so – they are a poetic and creative genius. The word 'genius' makes sense in the presence of Travis.

My dear departed friend was an epic Butch Dyke, a Black Butch Dyke, a Black Butch Dyke with a huge Harley. Beautifully handsome and proud of her intersections, she swaggered across town like no one I've ever known before or since. She holistically owned 'big dick energy' before any man even knew he had a dick. We hung out together for years when we were still young enough to get the night bus into the West End to go to clubs and the plethora of club-nights that sprung up in the late 80s and 90s like Taboo, The Mud Club and Kinky Gerlinky. We always thought of ourselves as West Enders as opposed to the other set who hung out in the East End. We'd laugh about being 'common up West'.

My friend, Avalon, was as butch as fuck but also as camp as fuck and proud of it. She was capital 'Q' queer.

She taught me so much about myself and about the stupidity of gender roles but also the sexiness of inhabiting them for fun. She told me I was trans before I was even ready to hear the word. She said it with love though, I know that. I miss her so much. As I walk to meet Travis, I think that I could cry here and now. I cannot believe that she is no longer in the world, our paths will no longer cross and she will no longer tell me over and over how proud of me she is. I feel sad but I don't want to feel sad as I'm excited to finally sit down and interview Travis, someone I have adored since seeing their TED talk a year or so back, a talk where they eloquently controlled their rage to form poetic words, phrases and paragraphs in which they talked about the acts of violence they face and how the single act of violence, the throwing of a burger for exam-ple, is magnified and intensified by the willful blindness of those around.

Avalon would have loved Travis and Travis would have loved Avalon, I wish they'd have met.

* * *

So you – specifically you, Travis – made me braver. I have to acknowledge that upfront in this interview. I also have to acknowledge that I don't think it's good enough for a trans person of colour to shelter yet another middle-aged white trans person. But it's true you enabled me to speak my truth louder and with more integrity. Your bravery – listening to you talk about the burger on Waterloo Bridge, that notion of the non-innocence of bystanders that you called out... Your tenacity and strength in that moment, and many others, made me realise that I had to speak my truth. It enabled me to say that I don't feel like a woman or a man, or even couch my transness in femininity or masculinity, but I can perform if I want. I want to open this interview with that. I do honestly think that trans people of colour are, as they have done for much of our history/histories, breaking new space and ground. We all benefit from this and we have to become far better siblings and accept our whiteness as pure privilege in order to become better siblings.

I wonder, do you think we'll ever get to the point where we can be undressed (perhaps through performance) and yet have the same degree of confidence we have now, or are developing? Will we ever be able to truly be trans and naked and confident?

Travis: No. I think to be undressed and have that confidence we'd have to first get to a place where the first thing we are told about our bodies is that they are not wrong, I feel like we are still stuck. I cannot imagine a world where the first thing we've done is something without our consent (i.e. we're gendered). I really believe that if that is still something that is happening, how can we undo the relationship that's given to our body from the get-go? From the get-go our body is in an un-consensual relationship with gender. I feel that even if we are trying establish our autonomy to our gender throughout our lives, it was born out of something that was not consensual. That tells me that our bodies start off from a bad place and I feel if that is happening I cannot imagine a confidence with being undressed. I want to be able to imagine it but...

What would it look like if we could imagine it? I know that's tough in our timeline as we are born into a dysphoric arena. (Not that dysphoria is the preserve of trans folk.)

Travis: No, we are just the ones naming it. Everyone's got body dysphoria. I feel like it would look like we would have more space in our heads to think about something else. If people wanted to think about their bodies, they could still think about their bodies, but we could imagine ourselves without them. But I think it's hard. I often say that a world without this would mean we'd all stop looking at bodies and then we'd all stop looking at gender. I sometimes get the response, 'But what about the people that want gender? Some people have fought for their gender and fought for their bodies so should be proud of it.' So, I'm like, 'Yes, but that's all still in relation to this world.' If there was a world without gender expectations and stereotypes, I think these people would actually be like, 'An arm, so what?' or 'My stomach, so what?' A piece of flesh wouldn't become such a thing; we wouldn't build all this history around bodies. There is so much writing around it: bodies being ships, bodies being temples.

I've been HIV positive for around twenty-five years now and people call me a 'long-term survivor', almost as if it has heroic connotations. But I survive because of drugs, because of chemical compounds. In other parts of the world where access to cheap or free HIV meds isn't available, is that body that dies any less heroic?

In the opening chapter of this book I talk about how, when I was a kid I used to colour-in my cock with my mum's lipstick to try and make it disappear, so 'boy' wasn't there anymore. I can laugh about it now, but actually the memory is of a really dissociative act that I performed on myself, which feels really harsh and makes me feel sad. For years I told people not to touch me there as I thought back then that, for me, being transgender meant being definitely female and cock-less and therefore I was going to wait for the 'vagina on a pedestal' until I could be touched or fucked down there. I wonder if we can mend that fracture within ourselves. I think so many of us believe that surgery will mend that pain.

Travis: Well, for me what happens in the conversation around transness is that first there's the 'I'm trans' declaration and then comes the assumption of physical change. Someone says, 'I'm trans' and the next question is 'When are you getting surgery?' or 'I'm trans. What have you had done?'

It's hard. I was quite nervous doing this interview because I'm someone who is very well documented online talking about their lack of need for medicalisation for transness, whilst simultaneously right now knowing differently and collapsing to possibly needing to get things done medically. There was a period when I used to want surgery all the time. I used to dream and picture myself looking very different to how I look now, and then life happened and my politics happened and things subsided. For the first time since talking about things publicly I'm finding public stuff really hard, because, if I'm honest, my politics are in direct conflict with what I'm now wanting internally, so I have to make some decisions. That's why I was really nervous about this interview; but I thought, 'I'm going to use it as a time to be honest.' I think part of the reason I haven't got stuff done (I could have as I've earned some money) is that I wonder, 'Am I getting this done because I think it will fix something and that assumes that my body was broken?' I think that's the issue surrounding trans politics at the moment: We don't have enough nuance in our conversation to say that it is completely natural or unnatural that you want this done to your body; and this is not to shame you. However, we do need to realise that this is not apolitical, this isn't some random choice to suddenly be aligned to this meta-being. No, this is happening because of violence and because we were told our bodies are wrong. This is happening because you were told that your penis can't possibly align to womanhood; that your hair can't possibly align to womanhood. I guess what I'm trying to interrogate is how we make these choices whilst knowing that there is something else behind it.

I felt really unaligned until I accepted that what surgery did and gave me was a reconfigured cock and balls, which has given me a facsimile of a vagina but using the best of me to create it. It helped to mend the brokenness I felt but it also feels aligned. Only us trans folk sculpt our genders to alignment. I do see my cave as being a work of art, a feminist statement, but I'm not out to make a political statement. I want comfort, joy and orgasms, but in order to do that I have to address my brokenness, which I feel like I do, but by embracing trans only and celebrating our capacity for change. When I finger myself now, I think, 'I wonder if that is cock or ball skin?' and I try to see if they feel different. I wonder if that helps in having a way forward because it's not about repairing ourselves for society and hiding our fault lines. I worry that historically our visible voices have only been older white women who may or may not have had male privilege, and that for many people now that old model of working towards being accepted by society at large doesn't work anyway.

Travis: It's just not that neat. I think that when you are oppressed on multiple axes – it's not an equation but when your life isn't as neat – then whiteness seems to give tidiness. I've never lived with white people, but as I have been around more white people, be they trans, queer, even if you're poor, there's something that's neat and logical about this – you have an ability to grasp something that feels logical about your narrative – and I'm like, what a luxury to think that this life is logical and what a luxury to think that life is this neat. I think about how I knew about castration, that I knew about changing my body before I knew about trans people because I knew about my great grandmother, about black women, the stories of how people in my family had to watch other people in my family be castrated. Now they weren't trans, but I think it's so white to think that the only people that are misgendered are trans people and that they are the only people who face body castration, body morphation, body changes, and body policing and misgendering. Let's go with misgendering because that feels like the hill that every white nonbinary person wants to live and die on. The idea that misgendering only happens to trans people actually comes from white supremacy. We know it is historically inaccurate because we have seen throughout history what happened to black men and women. Black women were put in cages because their bodies were failing at gender; black men were castrated, and their dicks were changed because they were failing at gender. And for me that tells me as a trans person in my family, in my family history – my family is African American – that even if I change this or that, my family were born in bodies that they didn't want to change, but the world still gendered them wrong, the world still treated their bodies badly. It's a very white idea that it's simple.

Does that create a kind of body memory legacy? I've been thinking a lot about the memories in my surgical space, the space they call a vagina. Nothing was added, except a concept. Everything there is from my life before. If it has an existing memory: it is of feeling shame, the memories of sex work in which I was being paid to be touched there, painful memories. I had to resolve that vibration of discord. I wonder how having your internal family memory and history informs your transness?

Travis: I think it told me that this wasn't going to be simple and that I couldn't just follow what I was seeing. I think if I was... well, I can't say if I was white, but if I wasn't racialised and born into a household that was heavily racialised (my experiences from a young age weren't *heavily* racialised as I was the lightest person in my household, but I grew up in extreme poverty and everyone around me looked like me but was darker), then maybe I would have transitioned in a different way. Maybe I would look different now because I wouldn't have the memory and the present recollection of things being messy and of violence being just about me. What being racialised from a young age taught me was that violence wasn't just about me. Violence was happening because of other things, and that told me that when I was figuring out my gender that meant 'hold on, this isn't just about me, this is about stuff that "they" have done'. I think that would be entirely different than if I googled 'trans' at fourteen. I would have seen 'I was born in the wrong body', I, I, I, I, I. That's relevant to some people, but for me, 'Hold on a minute, "I", but I think "them".' I'm not afraid to say that I don't think I would have always been trans, I think in another world I would have grown up being able to do the things I wanted to do and stayed calling myself Travis. The world forced a reaction out of me. It forced me to say, 'You need to change.' I just said, 'Pause, hold on a minute, what would that change look like?'

I sometimes think that when people talk about binary genders, only those people that had access to either or both with ease would talk about rejecting binaries, and get so caught up in the idea that pronouns alone will change or shift the world.

Travis: Now when people ask me my pronoun, I think, 'Can we talk about the real shit?' I'm not saying I don't give a shit about someone's pronouns. I do, but I worry about the other stuff, not just the fight for the 'they'/'them' pronoun. But what happens then? All the street knows I changed my pronoun yesterday, but I'm still here in a baggy hoody and jeans because yesterday I got a drink thrown at me and followed home in a dress and I don't want to wear that today. My pronouns haven't changed any of that shit here.

I was in a meeting last year which was centred on why trans people – some trans people – are so at risk from HIV and being diagnosed late. We had limited time, so we spent the first ten minutes sharing and talking about our pronouns. The room was cis and trans. I was shocked at how our time was taken up with our own sense of comfort, whilst talking about people – often brown- and black-skinned people – dying from AIDS. I sometimes feel like a lone voice... My head is interested in making change or at least creating the time for change to happen in.

What do we do to change this, talking about bodies as we want to without using almost fictitious terms?

Travis: I'm still figuring that one out. At the moment I censor so much of the stuff I say in the fear...

Why do you censor yourself?

Travis: I can deal with cisgender people throwing me out the pram but what I realise at the moment is that trans people in this country are feeling very heated up by the rise of TERFS [trans-exclusionary radical feminists]. I know that when the GRA [Gender Recognition Act] is done and dusted, the violence will still be here. Lots of trans people see this as the defining moment in trans history; it feels middle class. I'm not ready to be the one to talk out about this – not when half of trans people don't see me as trans anyway. I'm not ready for that backlash.

I'm so tired of being disappointed about others' politics. I've just got to make my show and make my work.

The word 'trans' seems to be owned by certain people and groups of people – it's quite academic. I just want to own my sliver. What's given me an opening to do that is being HIV positive, because I'm still rejected and treated badly by so much of society. My HIV outweighs my transness in terms of societal discrimination. I'm rejected because of HIV not trans. That ironically has allowed me to explore my transness apart from accepted trans norms. I have had to fight for my part of the word 'trans'.

How do we reframe trans?

Travis: I think how we reframe it is to sit down and wonder what our goals are as people and to decide what we want from gender. I think there are still lots of trans people who want and need gender to play exactly the same role it always has, and they are just happy they have got through it and to the other end. I think how we reframe trans is to centre gender nonconformity. By centring intersectional people, by centring people that are consistently existing outside of gender conformity, it will pinpoint where the violence is really at; it will pinpoint that actually a lot of this violence was never ever about transness but about not conforming the moment you go outside of gender's way. The moment you start to benefit from the privileges of the gender that you felt you always were is the moment you start conforming into it.

And adding to it, ironically. Adding to the very patriarchy that sets out to discipline us so harshly.

Travis: I really feel like…because I genuinely believe that trans is the majority and because I believe that everyone is trans.

I agree. I think we are immersed in living uncomfortable lives. Trans people are just working harder towards comfort. Most cis people I know live in degrees of uncomfortableness.

Travis: They will call it their job, their family, their kids, but deep down they know it is their body and gender.

I've stopped saying 'trans'. Now I just say, 'I'm living honest.' The word we use now is 'trans' but 3,000 years ago it wasn't the word they were using for people that look like me. So what feels truer for me is that I'm just being honest about who I am. It's you, the plural, that trans has had to equal: this, this and that… but actually, I'm part Filipino and have been researching gender nonconforming people in the Philippines – it's really annoying that, in looking back, these people are termed as trans.

I think we struggle to see trans away from a gender binary lens. I think our bodies often become a battle when they don't need to be. I have loved having surgery but I love that naked I absolutely have a proud trans body that doesn't satisfy or align with a binary structure. That feels like my power; my surgery feels miraculous in relation to my trans identity. I'm not chasing an end 'real' goal; we should be having a party, here and now.

Travis: As though realness was the objective.

So, for me, for an awful long time before I had surgery I felt like I couldn't really be intimate with people because of my genitals.

I avoided people going there. Of course I had sex, a lot of sex, and I worked in sex for a time so I would be lying to say I never had sex; but I always presumed that surgery would be the turning point for me. But actually after surgery I found it just as hard to work out what I wanted to happen. I had to rename so that stuff worked for me. How do you navigate this?

Travis: So how do I fuck?

Yes, I suppose.

Travis: At the moment I don't fuck enough.

I don't think any of us do.

Travis: I've always been afraid of penetration, so that's what I've noticed was very different to the way I wanted to have sex compared to maybe bodies that were being labelled like mine... Like when I grew up, people were like, 'This is a gay boy', and then I went into gay clubs and people were like, 'This is a feminine gay boy, a gay boy in make-up, so we're going to fuck them.' And I've never been good at that until I started with other trans people. At first, I was sleeping with just cis men (I started having sex at fourteen and was only having sex with cis men until I was seventeen) but then I slept with my first trans feminine person and I noticed the shift in what I was allowed to ask and the ways that they were allowed to touch my body. Before, I was very much focused on service, so if I was serving someone, they wouldn't have to pay attention to my body. I don't think I have an innate dysphoria around my genitalia, but what I have is a complete no relationship to it. So I'm fine if it's not paid attention to. I don't wake up and see it and say, 'I need to get that off me.' I just like it to be ignored. To me, sex had to go around that being ignored, which means I was okay being fucked if I was in a position where my penis would still be ignored. Then I think that through sleeping with trans people I didn't want it to be ignored. I thought it's here and I can receive pleasure from it but I need you to know that when you are working with it, it's a thing which feels separate. Even when I talk about it now, it feels separate so we have to work with that relation to it; like, so now, when I have sex, sex looks really vanilla. This isn't going to help me date. Sex has to look really slow now. And if I like it, I can have any sex I like; but it's about the sex I like now (I can get fucked but I just don't enjoy it). But it has to be really slow because for me I'm trying not to get rid of my penis – that's my goal. I'm like I don't want you to go but I feel that maybe we're in a losing battle.

I feel like I've got a relationship with your penis. In a sense that's how I felt for many years but, to be honest, I feel mine is still there. I had so much shame pre- and post-surgery about not fitting a script. But now I feel like I have been a really good caretaker of my body and my cock and balls. My cock wanted to not be seen and I didn't feel like I was ever male, so in a way the surgery was perfect in allowing both things to happen. In its new configuration it makes perfect sense to me. I'm not telling you or saying that you should or shouldn't have surgery. I'm just being honest with you. I'd been a two-bob sex worker for drugs and hadn't looked after my body. It matters to me now that I do care take my body – being a good proprietor of my body really matters. *I see surgery as part of that. Autonomy means we can make these choices. When you say you are taking things slow, it sounds beautiful, like you are in your own process. Do you feel a pressure to conform to a notion of what your body should be?*

Travis: Yes definitely.

I'm not sure I've heard a more tender thing as someone saying that they are battling for their penis in this process.

Travis: At this moment whilst we are doing this interview... I said it to someone the other day... I've only said it to a very few people, but I really want to find a way to exist as I can in this body now because I think I could like this body. But this is really exhausting. Can I do it? What that means is that today I'm wearing the least thing I wanted to wear today but yesterday I wore what I wanted to wear and the world consistently punished me from the moment I went out to the moment I got in. I felt like I can't do this anymore. I think that people think I tweet about the violence I experience but if I tweeted about all the violence I get it would be nonstop. And I think I am experiencing all this violence, so then I change my clothes – we're just talking about clothes and the physical body – and then I go into a room of trans people to try and feel safe and they say, 'You're not trans because you haven't done this, this and this.' And I say, 'Fuck, maybe if I change my body...' because I think if I had to pick, I think I can imagine myself looking like a cis woman. I can imagine myself with breasts. I can do that, that's not the question. But I also know that when I exist in this perfect middle ground I feel euphoric, I feel incredible and at one. Why do I need to go here to feel that? But then I feel pressure because I know if I made changes then the validity of my experiences would be listened to (i.e. my violence would be believed); but also, if I'm really, really honest, I sometimes look at my friends who have medically transitioned in different ways and I say, 'Girl, do you remember when you would wear that on the street, what you are wearing today, and the whole world would stop, traffic would stop, people wouldn't serve you, people would call you a freak and now you get a catcall at one point in the day.' People will say that is the height of misogyny but we know you are stopping traffic wearing the most boring black miniskirt and jumper, so there is a pressure for me to change my body so I can breathe. But, I know if I ever said that out of context people would assume it was because I couldn't breathe internally, when it's an external breathing.

We breathe really badly – we hold onto breath, we shallow breathe, we panic breathe, we tighten up. For me, this process is about finding comfort, to feel comfortable. If that means having surgery, do it. If that means having big tits, do it. If the world is doing it, then we have every right to find our comfort in exactly the same ways. But I also feel we can try to be slightly more than that because a lot of what the world does is really damaging, so we can move away from that or not just mirror. It must be awful to feel that you have these layers of violence so that you feel that violence doesn't end when you enter a trans space.

Travis: I just don't enter them.

When you perform does it feel safe?

Travis: Performance is for me the place where I can do the me that I want to be here, and do the me that I want to do on the street. I said this many times, but on stage I get applauded for the things they punish me for on the street. It's the only time I get recognition for the same thing I'm saying out here in a different form; and out here I'd die for it, but somehow trans body on stage becomes this, this and this.

You never go on stage and tell a passive tale of victimhood though. You're never passive – that idea that a trans person has to give everything to be liked and to be safe. I like it now when a cis person says to me, 'I've got your back.' I reply, 'Whilst you're there, fuck me.' They laugh nervously but it's about us being human and not a thing to be cared for in yet another paternalistic way.

Travis: They never desire us.

Can you see where this will resolve for you?

Travis: This is all very new for me. If we had this conversation six months ago I wouldn't have been saying this. It is very new stuff that is happening in my head. I think it is going to require real effort for me. My aesthetic for me is just the way I like to be. It's effortless, I love looking like a clown, like a freak, but I have never dressed with the intention of trying to look convincing at something. I don't know that game, so I'm calling up my trans girls and saying, 'Can you teach me some of those tricks?' I'm seeing what feels okay and what doesn't feel okay. I had a consultation and it made me feel sick, but not because I think there is anything wrong with them or the work.

Surgical consultations?

Travis: Yes, facial surgical people. Other people's decisions are not my business, and it's complex. I entirely respect other people. It's going to be really interesting because in ten years I don't know what I will look like.

It is about comfort, but let's at least look at what we add to patriarchy and think about the beauty standards we set and challenge them, even if we have work done and are beautiful.

Travis: I think what I know is that I don't need or want to get rid of my penis. When I imagine versions of myself in the future, I sometimes picture myself as this person that the world was seeing as a woman who was gender fucking a bit but had a cunt. Everyone was like, 'She has a cunt', but I still had a dick. Even in that version of myself, where the world sees me as a cis woman, I still had a dick.

I still feel like I still have a dick. It looks completely like a cunt, but isn't that the magic of it? Now all of you step out of the way so that we can show you how to make this world better.

Travis: There's such a moment in that because it is saying that I want a body that is trans.

A trans body is beautiful, desirable and courageous. It's a heroic body.

Travis: It's saying my body is not passive, our bodies are ours.

I feel like you have an epic voice, your nuanced understanding of what we are going through is so important.

Travis: If I could sum up our conversation here it would be that trans isn't something that we exit from, it can be something that we arrive into.

And stay there.

Travis: Yes, and stay there.

* * *

Talking to Travis makes me feel human and alive. I know that's an awful lot of responsibility to place on one set of shoulders: the responsibility of kick-starting so many of us up and out of our comparatively comfortable slumbers. Listening to Travis, it's easy to forget that they are only twenty-three years old, yet they have the wisdom, generosity, courage and poise of someone who has lived many lives, but not just any lives: important lives, creative lives, lives filled with laughter and lives filled with pain. Maybe that is the thing that Travis talked a lot about: their history and the history of racism, the history of being raised in a racist world in which being black and feminine or black and woman or black and man is deemed to be problematic and needing to be resolved for the sake of a white fragility which needs soothing...constantly soothing. Maybe it's that sense of history that has informed Travis's sense and view of the world to such an exquisitely poetic yet pragmatic level. Travis has the rare gift of taking often brutal and brutalising situations and making them art for others to consume. Travis's work makes me think about the war photographers, poets or artists, but then I remember that it is Travis in the thick of the battle.

Incredibly clever, subtle and full of nuance, Travis has done more than anyone else I know here in the U.K. to get their audience to think not just about the perpetrator of the violent act but about the silence and inaction of bystanders who walk by and who walk on. Travis defines a silent, insidious space on our streets, on public transport, on the way to work and on the way home from work, a space that is full of the potential for violence. Travis lifts the lid on that space, Travis calls out the people whose inactivity allows violence to bubble up and occur, but Travis also suffers terribly because of that space, a space they have to pass through day in, day out.

One of the things that comes up time and time again in my interviews is the people surrounding a negative event who look away, and how it is they who often hold the keys to creating real safety or challenging the kind of violence that Travis experiences day by day. The teachers that overlook transphobia or racism, the parent that says, 'Toughen up.' Transphobia exists not just because of transphobic people but because of the silence that surrounds acts of transphobia. Piers Morgan exists with a vast platform on which he can be vile because ITV remains silent because of the ratings. He is meaningless, they are structural.

The brilliant posters recently put up in Scotland which call out transphobia start to show us how we all need to become part of the solution, and not just online but also on the street, in workplaces and in our families. Especially us white people. Even as white trans folk, we don't have to deal with racism as soon as we leave the house.

White skin has a shit load of work to do in order to deconstruct and eradicate the privilege inherent in our own skin.

Our whiteness really does blind us to the violence that our very blindness creates all around. We create the shit that is so often thrown at Travis. But it's work we need to do because we are not blind; we are just enrolled in our privilege at birth in the same way we are assigned gender at birth down to our cocks or cunts. White skin privilege and cis male cock privilege. We as white trans 'femmes' have a key responsibility here to stop taking so much space – I've been horrified recently to hear white middle-class trans women in London talk about how they are the most at-risk group in relation to HIV.

Bullshit.

We have challenges, yes, the length of NHS queues, waiting times, pronouns on forms, and abuse on social media, but scratch the surface lightly of the data around trans women and HIV and you find black- and brown-skinned women from Mumbai to Rio being forced to live at the very edge of risk. An edge we only see in films or read about, or worse an edge we presume we experience as we wrongly pronounce their names on that single day of the year when a group of mainly, middle-aged white trans women come together to mourn the murders of women far, far away, whose lives we momentarily enact to grieve.

A candle for each one.

We have to be prepared to challenge racism anywhere and everywhere. We have to own our fault in this to try and do anything to erode this risk-edge which often means life and death, and which exists right here on our streets without us even knowing.

I couldn't debate or discuss issues with my friend Avalon without her patiently reminding me of our differences and how often my ease around a subject or issue was simply because of my white skin. I left Travis feeling the same, thinking that even as I deconstruct my journey, write this book and aim to rename my bodily parts and my processes, I do that with white skin and that gives me a sheen of protection in our society that allows me both access and some safety.

Even my HIV status is hidden in white skin.

Listen to the way people discuss HIV in Africa and then, say, HIV in Berlin. Listen to the words used to describe the risks that a white person takes sexually and then the risks that a person of colour takes. Nearly always there is a subtle difference in language or tone. I remember Avalon telling me that she had no option but to develop a tough exterior because, as the only black kid in her school, every day she endured horrible racism – not every other day, not occasionally, but every day. I have incidences of sexism, transphobia and discrimination because of my HIV status in my life, but not every day and nor do I expect it every day. I cannot imagine what racism must feel like, but if we want to change it I, and we, have to try harder.

It makes me think about Travis's book, *Before I Step Outside (You Love Me)*, and how in it Travis takes harsh experiences and packages them up as poems for us to learn from. Essentially, this should be taken as both an encounter with art and a learning experience. It is more than simple poetry; Travis is a wonderful artist and creative soul, but also they are one of the most incredibly generous human beings I have ever met. They take all of that spiteful, hateful shit that is thrown at them day in day out and, with a beautiful, dexterous, adventurous and magical touch, turn it into poetry, so that we, like it or not, the bystanders, can read about our passive cruelty and maybe, just maybe, understand the work that we have to do to detoxify the meaning inherent in the colour of our skin.

Travis's work (and they do not work alone, they work with others) is doing so much to push further and further into the distance the line at which we trans folk have to start jumping through hoops.

Avalon would have loved Travis. Avalon would have wanted to protect them as she did many of us. I miss her, I miss her strength and her humanity but I felt her spirit alive and kicking in the beauty and integrity of Travis.

KATE BORNSTEIN & BARBARA CARRELLAS

*I probably won't figure it out, but I'm tossing a pebble
in a pond where that ripple will reach someone.*

Kate Bornstein
Brown University, October 2018

I feel like I have nothing to say about the fact that I am about to interview Kate Bornstein and their partner Barbara Carrellas, because I feel stunned that it is really about to happen.

I always make notes before an interview and these notes are being made a couple of hours before it is scheduled to happen. In my head I keep repeating, 'I'm going to be interviewing Kate Bornstein and Barbara Carrellas.' I have a tension headache and I'm fighting a panic attack. I need to record this stuff; I need to remember this day.

Kate Bornstein and Barbara Carrellas... I'm overwhelmed, fucking overwhelmed. Bornstein and Carrellas: heroes of mine, practical and pragmatic heroes who have both, individually and (spookily) as a team helped guide me through the reconfiguration of my reconfiguration to a place of greater peace and ecstasy. I could cry.

I'm silenced by the prospect of interviewing Kate Bornstein, the person who enabled me to hold on to my life at a time when things felt impossible and wouldn't fit into the place that I had crafted for them over many years on my binary gender-journey. Kate Bornstein being in this world enabled me to feel some ease about myself, to feel like I might be valid at a time when I felt invalid and almost gender-journey fraudulent.

I cannot quite believe that I am about to do this interview, that somehow my life, in all of its past fucked-up-ness and messiness, has allowed me to get to the point where this kind of thing can happen. On one level this interview makes me feel spiritually complete in a way that much of the medicalised process of gender realignment didn't and perhaps couldn't.

Let me try and give some context to my overwhelming feelings.

Straight after my genital surgery I realised, when I was faced with the outcome of the binary exchange of my genitals from an apparent male to female model, that the presumed gender role attached to a vagina – female – made no more sense to me than the past gender role attached to a cock – that of male. I knew after surgery that I felt neither. I knew after surgery that I had an issue with gender that was beyond the binary. The feelings came out of nowhere like a huge swooping eagle with a lamb in its sights.

I felt like a solitary, odd fish out of water, recovering on a ward of trans women who utterly experienced the surgical process as being the last piece in a gender jigsaw: to them it made perfect binary sense. I envied the simplicity and comfort of their process. I envied the direct response they felt between the facsimile of the vagina to their womanhood. It was akin to being on a ward full of newborn babies. For them there was only simple joy. I felt like a truculent Grinch – awkward and not resolved.

Being speculum-prodded and then told their vaginal depth was either joyful or devastating, depending on their depth... But whatever the depth was, it made sense to them as they felt completion in their newly created cavities. It fitted with their notions and their ideas about womanhood. I was lost in the philosophy of my facsimile. The depth test interrupted, suddenly and without any politeness, my subtle and nuanced recovery to the hinterlands just outside of gender expectations and stereotypes. Being speculum-fucked felt instantly reductive and, for me, it simplified what would become my journey to my trans destination. It reduced it down to a level that only allowed me to disconnect and not connect. I felt failed yet again at gender.

I felt that someone had fucked me without my permission and told me a fact that made little sense to me as a clarifying factor in discovering and understanding my new gender status. The depth test ironically made me feel genderless and free, but also, at that time, quite alone. I didn't know the word nonbinary or fluid would have any application to me, I didn't know that my problem was the whole of gender. I'd presumed my journey would be simple: straightforward man to woman. I believed, like my ward partners, that I would leave that ward gender-complete. Finished, job done, vanilla woman output.

The minute after the depth test I felt lost, inextricably lost. Someone I admitted those feelings to told me I should look at the work of this person called Kate Bornstein. I found Kate's work on YouTube, first interviews and talks, and then through their written work – their books like *Gender Outlaw*.

Post-genital surgery I started to slip into the post-surgery blues but I was saved by one line from Kate, which stated simply how I felt: not man and not woman.

Kate Bornstein saved me because they quite literally showed me that there could be a context for me to grow within. I knew that I did not feel man – definitely not man, neither performatively nor inherently – but now I also knew that even after neo-vaginal surgery I did not feel like a woman. Finding Kate allowed me to stop feeling bad because I hadn't arrived at the place called 'woman' that I had assumed, for years and years, was the place I needed to arrive at.

I'd been preparing forever that my whole life would function around the word 'woman' – woman as my destination. I'd lived woman and dreamt woman, I'd dressed woman and judged myself woman against the word 'woman'.

Through Kate's words I started to know that my relationship with this thing we call gender could be shaped by me, to fit me, without feeling that I had to please anyone but me. I started to feel at home in my skin; and later, much later, when I could allow the psychosomatic rejoining of cock and ball skin to my newly configured genital space, I could actually start to flourish outside of normativity. Kate's work allowed me to understand autonomy and to not feel alone. Kate's words made sense of my surgery and my process to owning a trans body through trans confirmative surgery. Their words allowed my configuration to start to blossom.

Barbara Carrellas, author of *Urban Tantra*, has also played a pivotal role in my life over the last couple of years, especially in the way I have learnt to develop an intimate relationship with my body through both self-pleasure and the pleasure in learning to breathe more easily. Put simply, I have learnt to breathe more deeply and to acknowledge that, as breathing is the basis for everything in life, I need to do it well. I have had shallow- and panic-breathed my whole life in response to anxiety, fears and a sense of bodily detachment.

Through Barbara's work I started to understand that trying to be intimate and at one with my body meant learning how to develop an intimate relationship with it holistically – through breath, movement, response and reaction. It meant engaging with bodywork beyond the surgical, medical or the gender-reductive.

I'd demonised my body for being wrong, and then society had demonised it some more for appearing, to them, as broken and incongruent across its naked surface. It was a body of separate parts, all of which had created ways and methods of survival, none of which utilised the core strength – emotional or physical – that our bodies at best can offer. I'd learnt to survive in my body, a set of broken pieces in a toughened shell.

But I'd never stopped still for long enough on my shallow breathing to try and love and enjoy my body as a space I could rightfully occupy with comfort and joy. I'd never found it pleasurable, and therefore never wholly experienced pleasure within it, which is very different to just reaching orgasm or coming, which I had experienced many times. My body had become a protective space in which to hide and disappear.

Post-surgery, post-my acceptance of not being a man or a woman, I realised I could start to truly explore being present in me. Barbara's teachings and writings enabled me, through technique, to access parts of myself that would then allow me to lie down on the ground under my old olive tree, stay very still, my legs wide open, and feel the sun beat down on my genitals. I'd listen to the breath enter and leave my body. I learnt that if I stopped panic-breathing and focused on breathing properly and purposefully, then I allowed much more space and light within me. I realised that my body could and did relax. I relaxed. In my fifties I started to relax. For fuck sake, in my fifties.

Let's be clear here, I'm from Peckham, hardnosed and a natural disbeliever of anything that makes me feel vulnerable; but I trusted Barbara's words, as I do Kate's, and reading *Urban Tantra* I understood that in feeling cynical towards anything that I might wrongly interpret or perceive as spiritual – or worse, spiritual and middle class –I was only alienating myself from myself. Did I find any chakras or illuminating points of energy? No, but reading Barbara's writing, I saw that I wasn't being asked to. I was simply being given the tools to explore and feel. The sun on my genitals still feels like one of the pivotal moments in my life, when I truly awakened in my body and enjoyed my collaborative genitalia.

That gift from Barbara, the gift of just stopping and feeling the sun's warmth flood across my body, my genitals and then deep inside of me... It felt like ecstasy, a very intense form of personal ecstasy. I had a great orgasm like that, legs and lips open wide under my tree, because of the sun's warmth on my beautiful trans-genitals.

Between the two of them I feel quite beautifully tag-teamed, but also terrified as up to now they have been epic words on paper or images and voices on film.

I'm interviewing them by Skype. They're in New York and I'm in Spain. Normally I'd see that as a disadvantage because being in 'their' space matters. I always interview in person but I think if I was in the same room as them the interview would open with tears – tears of joy, but tears nonetheless, uncontrollable tears that wouldn't ever help the start of an interview. So an hour Skype it is. No tears, Juno, no tears.

* * *

I feel like talking about our relationships is so important in this battle-weary, reductive time of ours where we are left just fighting over words. It feels like exploring the richness and the difference in our day-to-day personal experiences – where you met, how you met, when you met – are vital. Yours is a fairly long journey and relationship.

Barbara: It's been twenty-one years.

I always feel if I can get to three years it's a miracle. Can you talk about those twenty-one years?

Barbara: Kate, what do you think?

Kate: Go ahead, Boo Boo.

Barbara: I'll start with how we met, and then we'll go there. I love the question 'How did it happen between you?' I was actually thinking about your three-year limit – I'm sure we've had many of those moments. Anyway, I was the director and the production manager for the performance artist Annie Sprinkle's show, 'Post-Porn Modernist', in the 90s and we were touring to San Francisco. I played a small role in the show, a bit at the intermission feature when Annie and I did a thing called 'tits on your head, Polaroids five dollars'. It was a comment on prostitution. I was the photographer.

Kate: Members of the audience would line up to the stage, wait in line – men and women, boys and girls. They would climb up the stage, still in line, and one at a time they would sit in front of Annie, who was bare-chested. She would put her tits, which were huge, on their head, and Barbara would snap a picture. That's 'tits on your head'.

Barbara: A Polaroid. A Polaroid meant that there was no negative, so only that person had that image. So at the end of that I would help Annie change her costume on stage, and she said to me, 'Kate Bornstein, the performance artist, is here. Ask her to come backstage afterwards.' I knew where she was sitting so I went up the proper aisle to the aisle seat where I knew this person was sitting and I said, 'Miss Bornstein'.

Kate: And I'm just sitting there not expecting anyone to approach me, let alone this really tall blonde, high heels.

Barbara: It was my high-class hooker look.

Kate: She had this great spangled jacket on, and I thought, 'Oh my gosh.' So I, being a gentleman, I stood up.

Barbara: And up, and up and up, and there's this tall redhead standing in front of me and I thought, 'That's very nice indeed.' I managed to mutter out my invitation for her. Kate was with her lesbian lover, who had just announced that she was going to become a man. They both announced they would come backstage and I thought, 'How fabulous, both of you.'

At that time I represented a lot of performance artists. There was a catchphrase, back in the day, in the 90s, that if there's a man in a dress or woman who takes hers off, Barbara Carrellas represents them. One of the few performance artists I didn't represent was Kate, because I'd heard she had a manager and it's not cool to steal a person from another manager. Very shortly after this, *Gender Outlaw* came out and that gave me her email address because she printed it in the book, the silly; but I always knew where she was, I'd kept an eye on her. I'd heard she'd broken up from her partner, who had transitioned, but I'd missed my chance – she had gone to be in a relationship with a dyke couple in Seattle. She came to perform one of her shows at PS122, and I flirted. It was nice but, no, she was still with the couple in Seattle.

Kate: Wait a minute, 'with the couple' doesn't quite explain it. I was their slave, their full-time 24/7 slave. It was a sadomasochistic relationship as well as a master–slave relationship. So when I got to PS122 to perform, I still had fresh scars on me. I was reminded of how deeply I belonged to these people.

That's such a tough bond, a blood bond. How can anyone ever come between that?

Kate: That show I was doing was a solo show with multiple characters. One of the characters was a slave girl who was telling the story of how she came to belong to this other woman and how wonderful that was, how she was branded. They were in a relationship for a long time, and then one day her lover says to her, 'I have to tell you something.' She took her jeans down and she was branded. It was like she was no longer a top. That is essentially what happened in my Seattle relationship; that's how I got out of it. I didn't jump out. I was attracted to Miss Carrellas but I was property and that wasn't the proper thing to do.

Did you know the deal in that relationship?

Barbara: I knew and understood the boundaries. By this point I was already teaching sex and relationships. I was uber-aware of those kinds of edges.

Fast forward to 1997. I am about to move to Australia to be in relationship with a cis heterosexual couple and to write my book and teach and just live there, I love Australia and have grown much of my work there. So that means I have to sublet my apartment, pack up all my stuff, put it on a boat and leave, and it was now midsummer. I was leaving at the end of summer – time was getting tight. I wrote to Annie (Annie Sprinkle) again, 'I'm desperate to rent out this apartment. I'm running out of time.' She said...

Kate: As that's going on there, I am in Seattle deciding okay I'm going to go for it, I'm going to move to New York and be a star. I packed up everything in a huge truck, and me and another dyke drove across country with my kitty and I moved to New York. I stayed with a friend but I needed a place of my own.

Barbara: So Annie says, 'I hear Kate Bornstein has moved to New York and I'm sure she'd need a place because she's only just moved.' 'Really', said I.

I email Kate. We talk.

Kate: And I said, 'Okay, let me come over and see the place.' I was dressing a little outrageously in those days – I was wearing what we'd call monster boots, with six-inch platforms, black spangly pants and a black tight top.

Barbara: And she had gone blonde.

Kate: Yeah, right. Sure enough we did talk and talk and talk and talk and talk some more.

Barbara: She rented the apartment within the first twenty minutes. The next five hours were about something else entirely.

Kate: I think importantly what intrigued us in those early days was my interest and knowledge of SM and Barbara's interest and knowledge of Tantra. I knew there was something the same here, something very similar.

Barbara: I did move to Australia. We knew we were in love but we were enlightened people.

How soon did you know you were in love?

Barbara: Like a week later. So we decided that we had a month together and that we would make the most of it, so we were going to go around New York being delightful, delighting other people. So in the day we packed boxes and at night we went out to be delightful, and at the end of the month I did indeed move to Australia. But when I got there the relationship broke up within five days.

Kate: Now we were staying in touch. These were the early days of AOL and CompuServe. We were staying in touch in chat rooms, live chat and we were having great cyber sex.

Barbara: Our favourite chat room (because, of course, it was against all the rules of whatever the server was, so we would meet in obscure CompuServe chat rooms) was an obscure legal one for legal topics. No one was ever in that chat room, except for one day when a law student entered and saw our chat and said, 'Excuse me is this the legal chat room?'

Back then chat rooms were completely open. It would need everyone to engage in cyber sex or no one. Words were very sexual.

Barbara: Then my work in Australia dried up. I was also there to produce Annie's next show, but due to obscure Australian laws that couldn't happen due to the content of the show. To cut a long story, I had to wait for my boxes to arrive six weeks later so I could send them back to New York.

If only those boxes could talk. Was it always comfortable, and if it was comfortable how was it? I remember those tough days. I was diagnosed around that time, in the very early 90s, at a time when AIDS was decimating so many.

Barbara: Congratulations, survivor.

Thank you. At the time I was given six months and I was offered death benefits. I was laughed out of doctors' surgeries when I tried to get help with my gender alignment. Any (so-called) elective surgery back then was deemed non-essential for those living/dying with HIV. But I remember really clearly the total ignorance around trans stuff, the complete lack of words even. The words 'sex change' were commonplace. How come in your relationship then there was never a barrier?

Kate: One of the things when we first got together was that Barbara was tied into a lesbian community and I said to her, 'You know if we get together people will revoke your lesbian status. They will tell you you're with a man.' That was pretty much standard then.

Barbara: I replied, 'I don't identify as a lesbian.'

What did you identify as?

Barbara: I don't think I did identify... Probably bisexual. Because I was in a relationship with a lesbian, I was part of a lesbian community. But Kate's remark didn't bother me because I didn't identify in that way. I had no skin in the game that way.

It was seeing your work, Kate, that made me feel okay about myself because I didn't feel like a man or a woman and didn't really feel that it was easy to pin my sexuality down to a point. Do you think, Kate, that we have moved on from those early days of trans ignorance?

Kate: Of course we have, but it's not universal. There's definitely a leading edge in the dyke world which just says 'fine', whereas sometimes the lesbian community tends to be much more assimilationist (though not all, obviously, as there is a leading edge there too). But bringing it back to comfort, I don't think that either of us were ever comfortable with each other; in fact, we say, 'Every day you do something that scares the hell out of me.' That's what kept me there.

Barbara: Yeah, for sure.

Kate: I had come to appreciate whatever it was that scared me in life, because there, in that direction, is some growth.

But that could be comfort. I don't necessarily see comfort as being all pleasant.

Barbara: I think you use the word 'comfort' in the way I describe ecstasy. It's not all pleasure. It, in fact, could be deeply cathartic and utterly transformational. I think 'comfortable' means something bigger in the way you are using it.

I'm definitely not talking about slippers and a cosy chair, more about being in the same pace as another, even if you are out of pace

with them. Maybe in a kind of synch? Living with HIV and death I
had to develop a comfort with it in order to survive.

Barbara: Kate?

Kate: You and I overlap, dear heart, in our closeness with death.
From my point – from high school on, from my mid-teens
on – I've been suicidal, I just wanted to die. There were several
attempts, there was always suicidal ideation. It wasn't until
twelve or thirteen years ago, when I wrote about it, and more
deeply when I was coming through chemotherapy and radiation
for lung cancer, that I began to embrace life. I'm still fascinated
with death – I can't imagine a more exciting experience – What
the fuck goes on?! I want to be as aware as I can be. I'm ready
for it, I can't wait, but, I can wait, and I can enjoy life now and
that's a big change for me.

What's that like, Barbara, to be up close and personal with?

Barbara: Well, I have a weird astrological conjunction that
puts me in a Scorpionic shadow world of death. In all my work,
sex and death have just danced together. But long before I met
Kate I lived through that AIDS crisis here in New York. I lost
over two hundred friends. I worked with people with AIDS for
many, many years. I went into Tantra and other forms of sacred
sexuality purely to help people through the AIDS crisis. Death
and I are really close friends. In the time we have been together,
Kate has not walked too terrifyingly close to the suicide line –
maybe more than once. It's not been a constant. I can appreciate
the dance and the intrigue. I can go there. I used to practise

orgasmic meditations where the whole purpose was to come as close as you could to experiencing death. I've been to weekend workshops that prepared you for death and allowed you to die.

I wanted to say thank you for all the work you did around AIDS in those very early days. I remember when no one would touch me. No one would come near me.

I was talking to Travis Alabanza a while ago and asked them about how we might inhabit bodies that society deems broken. I wonder, Kate, how can we get to the point of inhabiting bodies that are wrongly labelled at birth?

Kate: This is where I am going to go off on a fuck of a tangent. I, for the past ten years or so, have been getting progressively deeper and deeper into Buddhist philosophy – not religion but the philosophy and science of it – and when we talk of inhabiting a body we are saying, 'I'm a me and this isn't my body but I'm inhabiting it.' What Buddhists understand the self to be is body and mind, an aggregate of body and mind, and they take the mind into another four or five sub-units of what the mind actually is. There's consciousness, there's feelings, there's mental formations, but there's not something separate from body and mind. You can never find that, no matter how hard you look for it. So I think that when we talk about inhabiting bodies the language distances ourselves from our body. I can experience my body now, but when I thought I was solely a body or had to be in my body, that was very hard. I could be told that my body was wrong – enough people said that and I believed them for a long, long time – but if we believe that we are outside of our body and need to be in, we start to grab at it, we need to continually grab at the body: 'I have to get myself in there, I need to be inside my body, I have to do all these exercises in my body.' That no longer is a point of view that works for me. I find a great deal of comfort simply being aware that, yep, what I call me is a combination of this body and all the wacky stuff that is called my mind, and beyond that there's nothing else. So getting back to the idea of bodies being wrongly labelled from birth... You touched on labelling a body... The gendered body is very little other than the label, it doesn't exist without somebody labelling it, there is no gendered body beyond a label, so we can agree with the label, we can label it ourselves, we can insist that our label is better than someone else's label. But there is no such thing as a gendered body other than the agreement on the label.

But if a label is applied to your body before you can make any decision or input into that decision, we have to grow into a broken label. I tried to please my birth label by walking like a cowboy that I saw my dad watching in films. He liked Audie Murphy films so I tried to walk like Audie Murphy. I fell over a lot and became pigeon-toed. That was me trying to fit a label that didn't fit.

Kate: There's this sequence from birth: We hear what we're called and to one degree or another we agree or disagree with it. To the degree that we agree with what we're called, we don't think about it very much, it doesn't affect us; to the degree that we disagree and find out how that distances us from the love of others, we grasp, we reach out and think, 'I have to be what they are saying. I need to be.' Then we grasp and we grasp until we get a hold on it, and then we become attached to what we've been called.

For me, trying to walk like a cowboy.

Kate: Then we become what we've been called. We believe that this is what we have become. We identify. Once we identify as something we're called ('You're a man'; 'Okay, I'm a man'), then we never really stop grasping, because a big part of us doesn't believe it and it all feels broken and there are cracks in our persona all the time, even if other people can't see all of them all the time. Life becomes really frantic, all because we identify.

Barbara: I think this applies to fat, to learning disabled, too tall, nose too big.

Kate: American, 'I'm an American'.

Barbara: I'm not sure we are going to be able to live on this hopelessly crippled planet long enough to stop labelling each other. I don't just mean by gender, but I suspect that labelling each other by gender will be one of the last things to go. I hope I'm wrong. We might stop calling each ugly, stupid or fat, but I think it's going to take far longer to stop naming each other by gender. However, that being said, things have moved far more quickly than either Kate or I could have imagined. We do sit around and say we never thought we'd live long enough to see trans people being this visible in the world, BDSM taken off the list of psychiatric disorders, and sex work made legal somewhere in the world.

Kate: Parents embracing their trans kids.

Barbara: And certainly we never thought we'd live long enough to see gay people be able to marry. I could be wrong about the timeline here.

I think that a lot of the other stuff changing is dependent on gender binary, gender expectation and gender stereotypes being challenged, and being changed because an awful lot of the other stuff – body shaming, slut shaming, etc. – relies on patriarchy, sexism and gendered stereotypes. There's always a gendered edge to much of the problems in our society. I think gender labels have to topple in order for the rest to be impacted. For us to get beyond the shaming of real or unreal, gender needs to be challenged.

Kate what do you think about the word 'real'?

Kate: [Laughs] Fuck if I know! I guess for about four or five months I insisted that I was a real woman. It was right after my genital surgery – there was nothing to stop me from being a real woman at that moment. That faded.

I never felt that I could invest in gender; it always felt problematic for me. I dread the word 'real'.

Kate: When I was invited to go on a road trip with Caitlyn Jenner and six other trans women, I had to stop and think, 'Am I going to survive?' I was the only trans person there who didn't believe that I was a woman – I just didn't. Going back to before that point, growing up I knew I wasn't a boy – that never worked. I knew I wasn't going to be a man ever, but in obedience to what I was called and for lack of anything better to do, I pretended, I watched, I imitated, I pretended. That skill has made me a wonderful actor. Then when I went through with my transition, I watched, I imitated, I pretended, I watched, I imitated, I pretended, only this time to be female, to be woman. It wasn't until a few months after surgery that it dawned on me that being a woman didn't feel real to me any more than being a man had felt. Because of the belief in the binary, we end up being told, 'Well, if you don't feel like you are a real woman, then you're a man and you're not at all trans.' And you go, 'No, no, no.'

There is a really wonderful word. It's a real word and it's called 'polynary'. A binary is any phenomenon composed of two and only two parts; a polynary is a phenomenon that is composed of more than two parts. Gender is really a polynary, and once it is seen as a polynary then you can be real. Fine. You're real. I'm not.

So getting back to the bus and Caitlyn, the only way I could get along was to think, 'I get it: You understand yourself to be real. That means you are. I'm not and I'm not a woman, I'm a girl.' My preferred gender expression is cute. That's what I like and I'm a lady. I'm a lady as much as I'm a gentleman because those expressions and roles of gender are genteel and they smooth the road. They make getting along possible: 'Ladies and gentlemen, don't yell at each other.'

Barbara: In the theatre it's common practice to say in a company, 'Ladies and gentlemen, half hour.' It's both an honorific and a suggestion about how we should all behave towards each other. As such, it has always been two gender roles I have always been enormously fond of. People have said to me, 'You shouldn't be using those words.' And I've said, 'Fuck you! I like ladies and gentlemen and I don't care what genitals they have between their legs.'

For me it's like the word 'wank'.

Barbara: I like the word 'wank'. Actually, I have amended my ladies and gentlemen to 'Good evening, ladies and gentlemen and whatever else you are being tonight'. That is more inclusive.

I get that we are currently fighting a really tough battle for our rights, but it's incredibly reductive to be fighting over a single word or two words: 'real' and 'woman'. It feels reductive to us all as it posits woman or real as a static thing.

Kate: Again, the binary insists that there are only two genders: There are men and there are women. The kind of trans that people understand in the world today are people that were mistakenly called men and are now women, or people who were mistakenly called women and are now men. And that's it, there's no possibility in the binary for crossing that line back and forth, there's no possibility for straddling that line, there's no possibility for being neither; in fact, if you say 'neither' and break the binary that upsets everybody. That's what upsets people, so when you say 'I'm a real woman', then okay you are, and in the polynary there is a space for real women but in the binary there is only space for men or women. 'Real women' is actually a redundant thing, an unnecessary pairing of words.

I just use 'trans'. I like being a prefix to change and fluidity. 'Polynary' actually allows the inclusion of 'real' and 'not real' as states of lived

gendered experience, among many other states. The binary is so trig-
gering and a hive of dysphoria for everyone. Whilst we have to exist
in it, how can we stop that?

Kate: For me, how I've been able to stop that over the last couple
of years has been understanding the aspect of gender called
'gender attribution'. It's the aspect of gender where, when we
meet someone we automatically attribute a gender to them. We
never do it consciously: boom that's man; boom that's woman;
boom I don't know what that is. But again, because we have
to be one or the other, we need, grasp at and are attached to
'you must attribute the correct gender to me, here's my pronoun
and you better use it'. When we started this whole thing with
pronouns, I went, 'Alright, yeah, she and her.' When I was about
a year into my transition, my brother kept calling me 'he'. I blew
up, I was furious and I raged at him. He finally got it and called
me 'she'. But that was no life of peace – I wasn't being a lady.
And now, 'What are your pronouns?' I went from 'she' and 'her'
to 'they' (that was nice), 'zie' and 'hir'; if I wanted to get cranky
with people – and only very recently, really recently, and I'm not
expecting anyone to grab on to this – 'I don't give a fuck'. If you
want to call me 'he', that tells me more about you; if you want
to call me 'she', that tells me more about you. What you think
I am does not affect who I am and consider myself to be, but
gender attribution is a major part of gender, which has to fall
in line with the either/or of the rest of gender. So everything
becomes either/or: your gendered body becomes either/or; your
gender assignment is either/or; your gender role is either/or;
your gender expression is either/or; and your gender attribution
is either/or.

Our gender attribution has become weaponised to punish us back into a binary space. I'd love to fit neatly into nonbinary, but then it feels like I'm connected to the binary. Just being trans or using my name is enough to allow me some space.

Barbara: Let me talk about bodies. This comes off the fact that you talked about dysphoria.

In my workshops, particularly the advanced ones, I think that this is a lesson for everyone, but it has come through working with trans bodies. One of the cornerstones of my work is the erotic awakening massage, which is a combination of conscious breath work, conscious touch and extreme amounts of feedback. It's a receiver-driven erotic experience, and because communication is key and we are talking about sensation and not identity (i.e. a trans person/any person), we developed the trans version of the massage with 'How do you like to be touched?' I get answers like: 'Please treat this part of my body like a chest. If you treat it like breasts, it triggers dysphoria.' Then, for example, we move on to: 'Do that by being more up here rather than down lower.' 'Treat the head of my dick like it's my clit. Ignore everything else around it...and, by the way, I also like stroking and oil, and pinching, and long slow strokes and being teased.' Then we go on to talk about everything that isn't so body-centred. Sometimes I have found that when people have the space and are able to say, 'This is going to trigger dysphoria, so treat it this way', then they can release it and they can relax. We have agreement. I've picked binary examples for the sake of clarity.

Sometimes all it takes is that simple acknowledgement, 'I know this triggers it. Can we walk through this, this way?' Just uttering it allows them to move on.

It allows people not to live in a panicked sense. After reading your book, Urban Tantra, I focused on my breathing. I realised that I did it so badly. Just the simple act of breathing badly induces frenetic thoughts. I always try to be aware of my breathing in order to release the tension in my body of not being good enough. I don't have to breathe perfectly but just be aware of it.

Barbara: I think also the breath part of that process helps with what Kate was saying earlier: that sense that I'm not separate from my body – my mind, my emotions, my spirit and my body are connected, for as long as this earth adventure goes on; and I think that the breath is the thing, the glue, that keeps those things together.

Dysphoria makes us panic, and when we panic we shallow breathe.

Barbara: Maybe we can use it to better understand where our gender identity is coming from, feeling it as opposed to naming it all the time.

Our naming has been weaponised, as have our triggers. It's almost as if we don't have the words yet that create space. Kate, your writing and work have been key to me in terms of finding my own space. What do you think we can do as elders in our community/communities to enable or help to create more space that hasn't been, or isn't being, attacked or weaponised?

Kate: I see my role as an elder to basically provide some context. There are lots of ways to contextualise. We can contextualise in such a way to encourage an uprising, we can contextualise with the intention to pacify. My leaning is to contextualise with the intention to end gender-based suffering and increased gender-based happiness, and to that end I embrace another Buddhist principle: I attended a talk by the Dalai Lama – must be four or five years ago now – the title was, 'Profound Wisdom and Vast Compassion, the Essence of Eloquence'. More than anything I'd like to write a book like that, but I write books like *Gender Outlaw*. But going into this idea of eloquence, the Buddhist definition of eloquence is 'telling a truth in such a way that it eases suffering'.

You'll notice it's not telling *the* truth, it's telling *a* truth, because Buddhists understand that in our day-to-day world. I'm not talking on a profound spiritual level, but in our day-to-day world there are two kinds of truth: there's arguable truth and definitive truth. Definitive truths... There are not many of them; they are simply stated and they cannot be argued: 'Everyone dies' – you can't argue with that. Arguable truths... 'That person there is a real woman' – mmmm, maybe. And I thought, alright, is there a definitive truth about gender that everyone would have to agree on, whether they like it or not. I have my arguable truth of gender which I subscribe to because it eases my suffering and affords me some happiness and I had to go through several arguable truths of gender to get to it. But I found a definitive truth of fucking gender: gender is a binary, there are men and there are women, there is masculine and there is feminine, and this forms the basis of our sexuality and that's how it's been forever and that's how it's always going to be and that's the truth, arguably.

Arguably.

Gender is a polynary. There are plenty of ways to look at gender. You could be a man one day, a woman the next day. That person over there can be whatever they want to be. Your sexuality has nothing to do with your gender unless you want it to, and that's the truth, arguably.

The definitive truth of gender is much more simply stated. I've got two ways of stating it: the simple way and the academic way.

The simple definitive truth of gender is 'gender is relative'. The academic way is 'gender is relative to context and point of view'.

As soon as you argue that, you prove it. At that point you go, 'Oh yeah, that person over there believes that there are men and women and nothing else. Great. That's your arguable truth. It affords you an ease and some happiness. Have it. I bless your heart. Don't force it on me. Don't force it on my children – that you're not allowed to do, because it's an arguable truth and it doesn't necessarily apply to their context or their point of view.'

That's being mean.

I won't force my point of view on you. I understand that it's very upsetting to many people to think that there are more than two genders. Not everyone can embrace that or wants to embrace that. Letting go of grasping. As an elder, if I can pass that along I'll smile when I pass.

Barbara: Mine would be... Well, so many years ago I realised in the middle of some workshop where we were supposed to talk to our inner three-year-old or our inner four-year-old...but the person that kept coming through was my inner sixteen-year-old, and what my inner sixteen-year-old had to say to me was, 'You were right when you were sixteen – let's go back there. People tried to talk you out of it, you absorbed some of what they said or how they wanted you to be. Let's go back to the authenticity you had at sixteen.' So what I try to do now, especially with younger students, clients, colleagues, is listen and listen with the intention of giving them the opportunity to speak from that inner knowing, whether it's a sixteen-year-old or a fifteen-year-old, or an eighteen-year-old. That 'inner knowing what's right for you time' and when they can talk about it, say it and have it heard, especially by somebody older, reinforces their own voice back to them and displaces some of the voices that have got in between them and them, to quote you. And the upside for me is that I learn something. I learn something about what the world means for me now or what values in the world need to be supported. I learn what to support and I learn fascinating things in the process. Yeah.

Nobody listens when you're young. They think you're crazy, they think your impulse control isn't fully developed 'til your mid-twenties and everything you say is for shit. That's nuts.

I think listening is the most valuable thing I can do.

One of the key things that's happening at home now is the debate around self-identification, which has become really focused on young people. I was a primary school teacher many years ago. One of the delights of teaching young kids was listening to them dream up expansive worlds that they wanted to inhabit when they grew up. It was life itself in those conversations about flying to the moon or sailing to a far-off island where magic reigned over the land. If we just listen to young people, they tell us exactly what they need.

Barbara: What part of London did you grow up in?

East Dulwich and Peckham. I say to people that when we were young two sets of people knocked at our door: the police or people wanting to fight, and all I could do was to try and walk like Audie Murphy.

Barbara: Thank fucking god for you.

Thank fucking god for both of you.

* * *

After the interview with Kate and Barbara, I lay down.

I had to lie down and think about the space that they both create in the world, spaces they create with huge swathes of kindness and humanity. They both, in different ways, really touch the world and really touch me. We are living through such adversarial and violent times that it's easy to forget that there are myriad ways to respond to attack and to create a different, far safer world in which people's versions of their truths can be accommodated and celebrated, as long as they don't try to usurp or destabilise anyone else's idea of their own truth. It's simple really: Don't be unkind. Be kind.

Kate's world view is informed and navigated by first and foremost ensuring that people act with kindness and that no one sets out to be cruel or to hurt another person. At the same time, Kate manages to exist within an incredibly vibrant and radical framework which has remained radical and optimistic for many years. Kate and Barbara both possess a quiet yet determined optimism which fuels their radical work and words.

Barbara's world view, especially in relation to her bodywork, was formed during the AIDS crisis in the late 80s and 90s, at a time when people living with AIDS were shunned by society, by family and even by husbands, wives, partners and lovers. In those early years of the AIDS crisis, people living and dying with AIDS were physically rejected by the world for being wrongly labelled and stigmatised as dangerous and full of toxic blood which had to be shut and held deep within. I know, it was me, and I still ricochet silently from those early days.

Barbara's early work grew out of her desire to help to develop the ways and means for people living with AIDS to continue to experience touch and pleasure. Her feet are firmly rooted in that radical work and activism – not the kind that we might recognise on the street, but the kind evident in silent and intimate ways which focus on the body as a luxurious site of pleasure and needs. The need to feel touch, to feel present, the need to connect being alive with physical pleasure, whatever the context of hatefulness around. I know, it was me, and I still recall the dentist who gave me the last appointment of the day and covered the whole room in sheets of cling-film, me one side, human touch the other. I still remember me being the one to walk myself home, time and time again.

As I lay down to reflect on our shared time, the main thing that keeps coming back to me was the gentleness of the interview process, the gentleness of our conversation. Only occasionally did I, clumsily, snap it out of its beautiful calm and languorous 'happening' with my overly eager need to share and cram thousands of thoughts and words into the hour or so we had. They both operate from a place of quiet, unspoken acceptance that the way they work works. I get the sense that they know that they are helping, because they know deep down that they have helped many people already to feel more at ease. I am testament to that, testament to the work that their collective words and thoughts have invested across my bodily contours. Their impact on me is both life-saving and life-enhancing.

At several points during the interview I mistook Kate's contemplative silence for simply being silent. Several times I jumped in, struggling to cope with the silence. I adore being alone in silence or quiet but I struggle with collective silence.

Kate corrected me for jumping in and disrupting their thoughts, like a great teacher would: firm and definite, but still quiet; the peaceful atmosphere was entirely retained. I realised that my frenetic energy wasn't helping the interview. That's a tough but vital lesson to learn, especially midway through – what for me was a moment of art, creativity and lesson-learning. I stepped back from my energy and allowed it to hover and then fizzle; I had some work to do to get myself into the right space of mind to allow their words to emerge into the space, in the pace that they needed them to.

They're both incredibly nurturing and there is a sense of gentle generosity that in no way wants or needs acknowledgement.

As I lay pondering, I tried again to start to breathe more deeply and allow the content and feeling of the interview to wash over me. I want all of my ideas and my energies tied to my ideas to settle and to quieten down. To take my thoughts to the next level I need to try and regulate my emotions – somewhat, not completely, but enough to allow for better, more fluid flow.

Listening to Kate talk about their life – the extremes of suicidal ideation and attempts, their sexual desires in relation to BDSM, their recent illnesses and their thoughts about the potential of their legacy – it becomes clear that all Kate seeks their work to amount to is new safe or safer space. Space perhaps denied to them or space that they had to fight for, to become radical for, but space that they want others to enjoy from the get-go, if that is at all possible (Kate is an upfront realist). As radical thinkers go, Kate's work is remarkably open and accessible. Their language is the kind of language which aims to serve, to serve as a gift, a practical usable gift, a gift for activists to run with. It is not language to get lost in, rather language to be found in. What Kate demands for us as outsider queers are our own homespun comforts.

There is a perfect symbiosis to the relationship between Barbara and Kate and the ways that they work in the here and now, Kate seeks to create more safe space, new safe space for younger and older queers alike to be joyful within, and Barbara works in the here and now on the here and now, in getting us to enjoy the bodies that we might feel safer in. Between them they have concentrically circled so many of us over these past thirty or so years, providing us with a space that feels both fantastical and dreamy, a space by the warmth of a fire, a space with our legs dangling over the edge of a boardwalk, us laying naked on a beautiful soft quilt. Their individual and collective work is about those kinds of spaces, ones where we can breathe easily knowing that we have choices and that those choices are all fine as long as they don't hurt anyone else. The philosophy of Buddhism, and not the religion of Buddhism, runs deep.

They want nothing more and nothing less than for us to exist with rights, respect, dignity and a whole lot of fun. Even over Skype they both have great big naughty twinkles in their eyes that make me smile big and wide, and later as I draw my thighs together after a glorious wank I know that both of their energies have helped me get to this point.

HUSK & ROO

I've travelled up to Manchester by train with Michael, the Michael I interviewed in *Queer Sex*, the Michael who talked so beautifully about self-pleasure, about bodies-grown and non-grown and their sense of an innate masculine soul. That Michael is an intimate part of my life now. I was so utterly absorbed by their nuanced sense of their gender and the layers of performance they were prepared to encounter and contort, and the layers they simply shucked, that I instantly made contact after the interview. We've never stopped talking since.

Our friendship has grown from the complete excitement of finding another human being who thinks just a little bit like you. I never imagined I would find that...that I would find another person with whom I not only get lost in words and concepts but another person who would constantly challenge me to go deeper and think from different angles.

Michael's training as a therapist allows them a multiplicity of entry points to issues or objects, which often leads me to different spaces and starting points that I never considered. I am very Aries-like in my rushing ahead with a point of view and trying to make everything fit that idea or sense of something. Michael is much wiser than me and allows me to not only slow down but to reject and recycle my thoughts without judgement.

We are firm friends already. We haven't kissed and I'm not sure if we ever will or we ever won't, but their brain and their sense of them self is incredibly engaging and it is its own kind of attraction.

And I know it might sound trite to some, but the intimacy we share is based on a trust that comes from our working-class upbringings – we understand each other's fragilities, our fears of poverty and the importance of a secure home. We understand aspiration that isn't logical or linear because we weren't told how to become anything other than safer.

We also share a similar age; we understand references to music from the 70s; we both knew America in the 80s and 90s. It was Michael who introduced me to the wonderful spirit Barbara Carrellas and her partner, the legend that is Kate Bornstein. It is Michael who emotionally and practically supports me whilst I'm writing this book. I'm not talking about money here or actual things, but belief: They support me by believing in me as a writer.

I've never had that before and it feels luxurious to have someone really believe in you – not like a parent would from a place of blind love but from a place of support that nurtures creative growth. Michael is a soul I understand, I trust Michael implicitly. I've never had that before.

What a gift from a book called *Queer Sex*, this connection of ours.

We talk every week for hours about bodies, boundaries, performance, philosophy, class and our hopes and fears for the future and our futures. We are talking on the train on the way up, about the reason for the interview that I'm doing tomorrow with Husk and his partner Roo. It gets me thinking and looking out of the window through the fading light to the landscape beyond. Most of the interviews for *Queer Sex* were based in the South – not always with people from the South but people who now spend all their time, or much of their time, in and around London or Brighton. I wanted to leave London to interview people on their home turf and I wanted physical space and time on my journeys to them.

The journeys to and from my interviews are as important to me as the interviews themselves. Something happens before and after. It's something crafted from nerves and the unknown, and there's a sense of other lives I've been witness to. As it settles into my head it is at first jumbled and often overloading.

After an interview has been recorded and saved, the instinctive memory of the interview – the smells, the sounds, their mannerisms, and if they are two or more, their physical and emotional connectivity – all stay afloat in my mind and I try and make sense of it. Just very occasionally after an interview I still am not sure why it happened, why I travelled so far, or so early, or why them, or what the interview means in the grand scheme of the book. I like that feeling of not knowing. It's like I lose the label of interview and am left with the pure experience of meeting people, often entering their incredibly private spaces and discussing sex, bodies and love with them. I love talking about our bodies, our physical connections and how we fit each other and the world at large.

It can sometimes feel quite surreal, but always that surreal feeling is where the real space opens up and where connections and synapses start to be made and join up without my even sensing it is happening. So far the interviews in this book have all felt a little like that: surreal and beyond me. Writing this book feels like climbing a mountain with ledges twelve inches wide and drops of a thousand feet. This book is pushing me to know less and discover more. For a creature of habit that's quite unsettling but also joyful.

I've never been this happy personally or creatively. I'm lost in a world in which transness is the only currency worth having. Looking out of the window, I accept that I don't know why I am travelling up to this interview. I close my eyes and enjoy the nerves and anticipation which is bubbling up.

We arrive in Manchester on a warm late summer's evening, Michael tells me they know the way to the hotel and we end up looking up at a car park and down at the sat nav on Michael's phone. I think we are lost, but Michael assures me that we are close. We are. We just turn and face the other way, and there behind a row of trees is the hotel, somehow enormous but somehow hidden. In the first book I talked about a cry for help, I look at Michael sat across the small table in the room and think that they heard me.

Michael orders us room service: fish and chips. I steal their batter and reluctantly share my chips.

* * *

I don't really know either of you at all. I really wanted to interview you, Husk, after I saw you stand up and talk at the 'Trans Creative'

event in Manchester. The event was themed around my first book
Queer Sex, and you talked so brilliantly and bravely about being
a trans man with a vagina, which you are proud to use within your
sexual practice. I remember thinking how liberating it feels to be in
a room with people, young and old, who are talking so openly about
their transness and their bodies. I've not met you before, Roo. I wonder,
could you say something about how the two of you met?

Husk: We met at university. My university was really small. It
didn't have any halls of residence or anything like that, so I found
a house share. But, Roo, you'd already decided to move into this
house with all the people you'd met from the previous year.

Roo: We literally moved in together and I think it was about
four months until we got together.

Husk: I think it was that first December.

How long have you been together since?

Husk: It will be seven years this December.

Congratulations! When you met, how would you have defined
yourselves?

Roo: I think I'd have... It's a difficult one because now I identify
as queer, but I think back then I was using the terms 'female'
and 'bisexual'. Now I identify as female and queer.

Husk: When we first met, I wasn't out as trans yet. I was still working out what was going on. I wasn't one of those people who realised early when they were growing up.

So before you were in a serious relationship with Husk, did you have sex together?

Husk: Not together, but closer than friends. Roo was the first person I told.

Roo: I think you'd gone out and got drunk that night. Then I got a random text about one in the morning or something...

Husk: No, it was on Facebook chat.

Roo: Saying, 'I don't know how to say it but sometimes I feel like a boy.'

Husk: Is that what I said?

Roo: Yes. I just thought, 'Okay, sure.'

Was it as easy as that? Were you already in a relationship?

Roo: Not really. We were friends, flatmates.

Husk: I think for me I was in a really delicate place, I didn't have the energy for a relationship. I was in the excitement of change, university, and all the gender stuff.

How did you go from that to then being in a seven-year relationship?

Husk: We were kind of together, but nothing was said.

Okay, so by then you were sleeping together, having sex?

Both: Yeah, we were.

Husk: Yes.

Roo: Yes.

Husk: It started because we went for naps in the middle of the day, and then the naps became more energetic.

This isn't a guide book, but I think it might be really useful if someone could pick this book up and think, 'I'm at that point and I fancy this person or that person', but doesn't believe it could ever be that easy. Was it? Did it just work?

Roo: It just happened.

Husk: I think I instigated it. We didn't talk about it, but I felt really comfortable. Roo had said that she was bisexual, so that felt okay.

Roo: It definitely felt easy.

Husk: Roo had said that she was comfortable with my body and I felt comfortable enough with her to be comfortable enough with my body, and then it just felt easy.

So that was pre any medical interventions, hormones?

Husk: Yes. I didn't even use a binder at that point, It was really early in my process. I hadn't started any physical stuff.

Did you know what to expect?

Roo: I didn't really. He said that he didn't know if he would get anything done. I didn't know any other trans people at all. I didn't really know what it meant. I hadn't experienced a person who was trans before. I think I just accepted him for him, rather than thinking about gender.

It's such a different time. It sounds like for you it just wasn't an issue. It sounds wonderful.

Roo: From me knowing him before he came out to him saying, 'I'm trans', nothing about him deep down changed. His personality was still the same.

Husk: As my body started to change, there were things you said – like, I remember before I had my chest surgery, you said that you were going to miss my boobs!

Roo: But now I don't even think about it.

What an incredibly tender but also honest thing to be able to say. When I go to interview people, I never really know what they are going to say. I maybe have a hunch about the direction of the conversation, but things are always surprising. The tenderness and love between both of you is obvious and lovely to see. I feel honoured.

There is a beautifulness to both of you and to your relationship. It inspires me. As Husk changed, Roo, what was that like? It must have been a process that you both went through?

Roo: Throughout all of our relationship I wanted him to grow. He really wanted a beard, so he talked about needing testosterone. The first time he got testosterone, he left it on the table for me to see when I came in from work. He was so excited, and I was for him.

Was it an injection?

Husk: No, at the time I used the gel, but that didn't work well for me.

It didn't give you the beard then – that's a great beard!

Husk: It's not quite there yet. No, it didn't give me the beard but the gel did make my voice drop a bit and made me put on weight, I became quite chubby.

Were there times, Roo, where you loved being in this relationship because your partner was trans? We never really celebrate transness in a relationship. It definitely used to be seen as second-best, or the one 'you can't take home'.

Roo: I think it all the time now. When I meet people, I can't wait to tell them. I feel incredibly lucky. It's actually cool.

Husk: I'm the same. I say, 'Hi, I'm Husk, I'm trans.'

I think we are here to make this world a better place. We are the party that's taking place, even if they don't recognise it yet. I love our transness.

Husk: I've had a little bit of lower surgery. I've still got my vagina, but when you take testosterone your clit grows. I've had the first stage of metoidioplasty. Do you know about that procedure?

Can you explain it?

Husk: There are a couple of different surgeries to create a phallus. One of them is phallosplasty, where you end up with a traditional-looking penis. The other one, metoidioplasty, is the one I went for. It's where they use what you've got – the growth that you've got – and make a micro penis. The first stage is that they release the clit, so that it hangs more realistically – more phallic, less clit. I was worried about having that because I was worried about Roo's reaction, but she told me that she really likes it and doesn't really like penises.

Would you be happy if Husk had a phallosplasty?

Roo: The way I see things now is that not anything major about him is changing. Husk is still Husk. His personality stays the same. What makes him happy makes me happy. There are a million ways to have sex. I sometimes think that it is other cis people who really have the problems.

Does it free you up, Roo, in terms of gender and gender expectations?

Roo: Definitely. I've always identified as female, but we've talked about what if I wanted to change? Then it would be fine. It's like I have the space to explore.

Is that the depth of your love, do you think?

Husk: Yes, absolutely.

Roo: Yes, I absolutely know our love and relationship would carry on.

I've only known you both for a few minutes but I can see it would. We spend so much time having to fight, but it's really this simple, just like love.

Husk: Sometimes it feels like us against the world. Some of our friends don't understand. No matter how much some of them love us, there can be a barrier to understanding our relationship.

I don't get it. I just feel love, no barrier. I feel like I'd have to really put a barrier there. That would be a lot of work. All I see is two young people in love. How old are you by the way?

Husk: I'm 25. Roo is 27.

Did sex evolve? I'm not asking about the intricacies, but has it evolved as your bodies evolved?

Roo: Definitely. The fact that Husk has a micro penis now is entirely different to him having a clit.

Husk: For me the sensation is completely different. We met before T, so my body's sensation has completely changed and we have been through the whole process growing together.

Are words or labels for your body important? Is it 'dick' or 'clit' or something entirely different?

Husk: I don't really care. We call it whatever, usually 'willy' but I don't care if it's called 'dick' or 'clit'.

I'm just trying to give away words until better ones come along. If I use 'vagina', it feels like an odd vagina, but if I say 'my trans cave' it is just magical. I love the idea that your willy is so carefree.

Husk: We've started to use the word 'nub' as well, quite recently.

I love the word 'nub'. I feel like trans is the very nub of me. What does sex feel like for you? Can you explain it in words?

Husk: We both come. It feels queer, un-heteronormative. It seems like others have really unsatisfying and closed sex. We talk, explore, and if something isn't working we leave it and don't feel bad. We can laugh about stuff. It's not linear. Because I know we are both queer, it's like we have the space to talk and the trust.

How would you define your sexuality?

Husk: Queer. It moves and shifts and includes the different gender elements. I don't identify particularly with binary gender.

Do you both fuck?

Husk: Not very often. We explore most other things but not penetration. If there was, it would be an accessory.

Would you be top?

Roo: No, we'd take it in turns. Husk is proud of having a vagina and being able to use it. There's no shame at all.

Husk: Having a vagina is kick-ass.

So you have no assigned roles?

Roo: No, not at all. Not sexually, no. We both fuck equally.

How come you are so liberated, Roo, from all that gender stuff?

Roo: I think it has to be my parents. They were really open and stuff.

Husk: They are nowhere near as open as you though.

Roo: I suppose, but from the time I went to school if I heard other kids saying problematic things, I would go home and say it to my mum and she would explain it to me and tell me about how unkind things can be. It allowed me to develop real empathy I think.

Can either of you imagine anything better than this relationship?

Roo: No, not at all. We help each other to learn and grow. Literally, it frees us both up. I utterly believe that we all exist on a spectrum and that if I needed to shift I could.

Do you ever play around with this?

Roo: Yes, I often bend him over playing.

Husk: I love not being pigeon-holed. I know I look like a tough musician type who works out, and I'd hate to get boxed in by that. This relationship gives me space.

Roo: You are really feminine.

You have such a great relationship with your body - your vagina and your dick/willy. There's no shame and little, if any, dysphoria. How come?

Husk: When I thought about how I wanted my body to change, it was never anything to do with my genitals. When I did decide to make some changes, I knew I wanted to keep my vagina. It always felt simple and straightforward.

You feel entirely comfortable being fucked?

Husk: Yes, of course.

Does T change what you want to do?

Husk: No, it just sometimes changes how fast I want to get there, depending on when I have T.

Can you penetrate with a micro penis?

Husk: I can't, no, but it's not really something we desire. It's not an aim of mine. We have talked about strap-ons and stuff but probably more for my benefit.

Roo: For me to fuck Husk.

How perfectly matched you are. Do you realise how perfectly simple and happy you make trans? Your story proves that you can have as much or as little surgery as you want, be happy in your body and that there will be someone perfect for you. Could it be more perfect?

Roo: We could get married.

Husk: We are engaged.

Roo: We don't want kids at this time, just kittens.

Your kittens are going to be so loved. You're both cracking. Thank you, and please invite me to the wedding.

* * *

The interview with Husk and Roo took place in the most uncomfortable space I have ever had to interview in. I think it was a boiler cupboard, the kind of space you would have hidden in at school to have a sneaky fag or to kiss someone. I kissed an American boy at school in a cupboard like this one. He, being

American and all, was declared the school jock but he also loved kissing boys as well as the girls. He wasn't a great kisser sadly, but it was one of only a few tender memories I have from my school days.

The interview room was the kind of space I hid in when I bunked lessons at school. I hated being at school and spent lots of time in that cupboard or walking out of school and hanging out on my own.

I felt like a fish out of water for most of my young life. I had no words for me or words for the space that existed between me and the world. From my teens onwards I turned to sex and drugs to try and fill the void – often sex I didn't really want or properly consent to, but sex I didn't feel when it hurt, because I wasn't really inside my skin. If I was inside, it was so deep that dermal or emotional pain didn't penetrate and seemed to exist only on my surface. I was wrong. I was young, naive and desperate to feel part of the world. The pain did work its way down to me and stayed there, untouched as memories to contend and deal with later when I could.

I was called a sissy and a poof most days at school. I had to develop a barrier against the incoming pain, a way of trying to lessen the attacks and to fit in. External dysphoria, which name-calling created, is different from the internal dysphoria that I felt, which made me look at my cock and balls as not being mine and made me not understand my gender alignment. That made me colour-in my genitals.

The internal dysphoria hurt, but the external, applied dysphoria – never pleasing them, never fitting in, always standing out – made me take risks in order to be accepted and liked. I accepted lifts from strangers who smiled at me and ended up in locked cars.

The internal dysphoria was actually much more engaged with my body and my sense of self. Somehow there was a dialogue between what I wanted to be and what I wasn't. But the external dysphoria which pummelled my skin every day from the outside made me crumble in situations of stress, fear or panic. I stopped breathing. I was raped. By the age of sixteen I'd become immune to external pain. Nothing hurt anymore. I believed, as society told me day in and day out, that I was broken and deserved no more than this. I lived up to the dysphoria that they applied.

It took me years to breathe out the pain of being raped. Society owns dysphoria and applies it to us at birth when it deems us broken and unworthy bodies, not gender aligned and sometimes not gender specific. Of course I ended up in dangerous situations woven from risk, because I was constantly being told I was already a broken idea of a person. I distinctly remember hearing someone say about a 'sex change' person who lived near to us that they would be better off dead.

I lost over ten years to drug addiction and the ensuing therapy before I realised that society was broken in relation to gender, and not me. I was raped because society deemed me unworthy as trans from birth, a sissy, poof, effeminate and girly, and therefore didn't notice when I was at risk on the outskirts of town. I was desperate to feel the feelings and emotions that those around me seemed to feel without trying or having to try.

Society puts up a wall between trans folk and the world and then only seems to respect us if we somehow smash our way through and then remain silent and compliant on the other side.

Fuck that shit.

I cannot bear the thought that any young trans person will waste the years I wasted and take the risks that I took in the hinterland between my skin and the world that constantly rejected me.

Fuck that.

We should be supporting young trans people to transition, socially and medically, as soon as they declare their authentic truth to the world. I know I was raped because no one was looking. No one took that much notice of the broken kid, because they were already broken, right?

Fuck. That. Shit.

Talking and listening to Husk and Roo, I recognise two young people whose lives have come together with authenticity and truth in their naturally lived timeframes, and by that, I mean that they haven't wasted years in unassigned, uncomfortable gender roles and gender relationships that don't fit and are forced on them. They are on track to live happy lives, and in doing so they smash the patriarchy ever so gently along the way without needing to say it. And in doing so, they free up all of us.

There was so little dysphoria in that small hot room that it makes me cry happy tears.

Husk and Roo allowed me to reconnect with the unhappy child I was and to hug them tighter and to tell them that they've done alright.

I seldom ever mention the people out there determined to stop self-identification – those who question and disbelieve the young trans folk simply wanting to be themselves – but to them I simply say, 'You have blood on your hands and the world will write you down as being part of the systemic problem that forces trans folk deeper into the dysphoria that you force upon us when you try to curtail our naturally felt authenticity.'

'I see you. I see your spitefulness for what it is. You can dress it up all you want, but I see you and I'll never forgive you.'

JOSEPHINE JONES & RUBY

This book opens with a lovely quote from the legendary April Ashley. I am so thankful for her words. They are like gold dust to me.

It felt vital for me to have those words present in this book and to acknowledge and connect our histories, to see all of us as part of the same lineage, however differently we might talk about or define ourselves then or now. I wanted to honour our elders who have gone before.

In 1960, a few years before I was born, April underwent what was then called 'sex reassignment surgery' or a 'sex change'. It was life and death stuff, full of risk and complications. My mother was just twenty at the time of April's surgery, married with one child already (my sister, born in 1959). April and my mum are of the same generation: women who had to fight for space, be they trans or not-trans; women who have fought patriarchy their whole lives.

April says that after she came out of surgery from the clinic in Casablanca she fell down in the gutter, screaming with laughter. She was so happy that she couldn't stop laughing.

Trans ecstasy.

What amazing elders we are honoured to have in our trans community. Every one of them is epic, be they transgender, transsexual, man, woman, nonbinary, fluid, masculine, feminine or anywhere in between. They will have fought hard, day in, day out, for our freedoms. They lived at the coal face of discrimination and the fight for equality without any wriggle room unless they completely hid their truth from sight, and then they risked being brutally outed.

I acknowledge them in all of my current definitions for myself, as I give away the words 'real', 'woman' and 'vagina'. I do so knowing whose shoulders hold me up high enough to have some safety.

Brave warriors, they enable me, many years later, to describe my surgery as 'trans-confirming' and to describe my genitals as 'trans-genitals'. Without April, her epic dignity and strength, which helped her to endure the attacks, the headlines, the zoo-like public curiosity, I wouldn't be here now with the freedom to write this book. I don't just owe her my legal rights and my legal dignity; I also owe her the rights I now have to redefine my transness as being so utterly different to hers; I owe her for my being able to explore trans as the destination and not, for me, womanhood.

It took April from 1955, the year she moved to Paris and changed her name to Toni, until 2005 to be able to officially and legally change the gender on her birth certificate. Fifty years of society structurally and systemically treating her as an anomaly and as a gender freak. Fifty years she put in for us, fifty years of trans service. I'm only at ten.

I dedicate this chapter to April Ashley and my mum!

I'm in Bermondsey, specifically South Bermondsey, near to where my mum last lived in London. My head is full of the April quote – I received it by email this morning and read it to my mum. I'm thinking about the quote, about my mum's life, and by default my own life as I walk through these familiar streets.

My mum has always had fantastic short hair and great legs. 'Dancer's legs,' she said, 'from years of ballet as a kid.' In the 60s and 70s I remember people saying that because of her legs she looked good in anything, and that she could throw anything on. She loves clothes and gardening, growing everything from seed, with trays of seedlings all over the house on every window ledge. And she always wore shoes, bags and belts that matched. She has a great aesthetic: bags, shoes, belts and flowers, masses of cottage-garden flowers.

She's always inspired me, although now she despairs with me because I define myself as trans and not as a woman. She still worries that I'd be safer and happier if I just fitted in and played the game. She knows it's a game. People accused her of not being the 'right kind of woman' for years simply because of her determination to live her own life. She dug her own garden and ran very rough pubs. She still always calls me 'she' and 'her', but not only is that okay, it's full of love, despite my feeling as little like a 'she' as I did a 'he'. She accepted me and accepts me as I am, and did from day one. No question.

I feel nostalgic and a little sad walking through Bermondsey this morning, probably because my mum is getting older and the days of my mum living in this part of town are fading. I miss those days. We seldom get to hang out in the same way that we once did. People sometimes say that as your parents get older they become less emotionally, and definitely less physically, available. It's selfish and childish to want them to stay the same, but this morning I do.

She remembers the headlines around April Ashley in the 60s. We talked about it this morning. She said it was so shocking at the time. It must have made her terrified about my future when I first came out to her in my early thirties. That public trashing of trans lives was, and still is, commonplace.

Josephine Jones reminds me of April Ashley and reminds me of my mum's ballet legs. I don't think that is the only reason I'm going to interview her but I do love the connection they have for me across many years. It feels like a journey for my mum, for April and for Josephine.

I met Josephine at Trans Pride a couple of years ago. For some reason that day it struck me that the different generations of transness present had all found their comfortable places in the park – their tribes so to speak. It was like we had all gathered on the Serengeti Plain, small prides of different animals: giraffes, hyenas and lions. Josephine walked by like a gazelle in her own charismatic mist, blissfully unaware of how she seemed to exist out of any timeframe. She had no tribe.

A model and fashion designer who embodies the feminine and who exudes the kind of languid potential that always leads to great creativity and art, Josephine is tall and slender, reminiscent of the models in the 60s such as Jean Shrimpton and Twiggy. Josephine has modelled for Chanel in Paris and shown her own collection at London Fashion Week. She is a woman, a trans woman on the cusp of a brilliant future.

As I sit down awkwardly on a large cushion to interview Josephine, who is in front of me lounging on a faded pink velvet sofa, looking utterly divine, I realise that I never inherited my mum's great legs. Mine are short London legs that I tuck under neatly and we get started.

* * *

I don't really know a lot about you. I met you a couple of years ago with friends and I was completely bowled over by something about you: charisma.

JJ: I've just turned 22 and I am from where the roses grow in Buckinghamshire, but I'm an orphan. I live in London now, that's my home. I've just graduated with my Fine Art degree from Goldsmiths and I'm a fashion model. I've also just set up my own boutique.

So you have just turned 22. When did Josephine start? I'm not asking a before or after question, but as you sit here now there is a confidence and fabulousness to you. So when did you start to inhabit that?

JJ: I've never not inhabited that space. Some people may perceive this space as performed, or constructed or labored, but I enjoy the physical space of thinking about aesthetics and I love clothes – vintage. I think I've always worked from an internal resonance of what I find pleasing and beautiful. It works with who I am. I seldom think about my gender. Style outweighs all for me. There has been a feminine essence, I'm not about to get into gender essentialism, but there was never a binary switch. This was always me. My dad asked me when I was seven, I think, if I wanted him to take me to Thailand as he knew what I was, even before I understood (but he knew). I scream now back at myself, 'Josephine, say "yes".' I was always the one in the dressing-up box.

Were your parents liberal and supportive?

JJ: They were very bohemian, atheists. It wasn't a problem, they just wanted me to be happy.

Do you think they understood?

JJ: I think they had a premonition, there was a tension. Why wouldn't there be? I was very different. I've always been Josephine. The name change was just a formality. I've always been on this journey. There has been no demarcation apart from maybe choosing the name. We are all evolving personas – all of us, trans or not – and I object to it being an issue.

I tell people that I was simply born trans.

JJ: I'm not searching for feminine as an end goal. I feel that femininity has been resonant with the space I love and inhabit. It's not a chore – I don't have to do any work to enjoy that space. But I'm not ashamed and I refuse to give up certain masculine elements that have worked for me. I do have a certain brashness that works for me in modelling. Women aren't encouraged to develop that baseline confidence. I feel slightly embarrassed to say that.

I find it interesting that you say about feeling embarrassed because as trans folk we are almost taught that we must divide everything up resolutely to be masculine or feminine or declare ourselves as fluid, queer, nonbinary rather than challenge the dividing of language and personal traits such as brashness as being masculine. It's like we are expected to commit to a 'femme' journey or a 'masculine' journey. Shouldn't we aim for greater confidence?

JJ: I just wonder if it pertains to a masculine childhood.

Is this a product of a loving childhood or a product determined by patriarchy?

JJ: I've never been very good at reality. My skill-set exists in fantasy, be that styling an editorial or creating a look for myself. I can link that to my transness – not as escapism but as freedom. I think I inherently resist the gender binary because it's something I've never welcomed. I am often asked if I am rebelling against it through my transness, but it was never something I welcomed. It's not conscious.

When my surgeon did the depth test on me after surgery, I knew that I rejected the structures of sexism that said I would be deemed a success by the depth of my cave. Like it was a measure of my femininity. How do you describe yourself?

JJ: I describe myself as a proud transgender woman. That appeases and allows me shorthand. It's digestible. I don't spend a lot of time thinking about how I am perceived – that is probably due to a certain passing privilege. I recognise that privilege is allowing me space. But I feel if you can afford yourself that privilege to not focus on it, day in and day out, then it's an act of care. As a woman, as a feminist, I was spending every day thinking about it and it became an act of punishment thinking about the degree to which I was perceived as being feminine. I made complete peace being a trans woman. I no longer berate myself.

I always found the performance of woman or man tough. Trans fits me without that struggle.

JJ: I completely disagree. I don't find performance tough – that's my currency, that's what I do. I love that. I think if performance comes naturally to you, then it doesn't make you a bad trans woman or man. I fucking enjoy performing. I'm inherently drawn to it.

How does that fit into your modelling?

JJ: I love the art of dressing. I think that's what I'm about. Clothing has a language and I want to be fluid. My performance isn't considered. People might apply that to me as a model who is trans. I never wake up and think 'I will perform.' My yearning to be glamorous is my authentic. If I were to be any other way, it would be inauthentic.

I only ever performed trying not to be trans. I used to try and be a cowboy to please my dad, who loved cowboy films. I became clumsy and often fell over. I became the clumsy kid. Having performance confidence is a real gift.

JJ: I never want to please others but obviously I need to fit in because as a trans woman it avoids violence. I'm not completely oblivious to the world outside of my fantasy, but it's such a waste of time for me to be anything other than myself. I'm sure that comes from my mum allowing me to be myself and dress up; not that it was overtly encouraged but I was still allowed the space to develop. I would lose the battle in trying to please others.

Do you use modelling as a space to develop within?

JJ: I think the transformative nature of clothes allowed me to hide a body, pre-hormones, in avant-garde shapes. I viewed my body pre-hormones as not feminine enough. It wasn't a struggle though; it felt natural.

I read something by you once in which you said that you 'were enjoying how hormones were changing your body to allow you to feel more at ease'. I think you posted it with a photograph of you modelling on a railway platform. I've paraphrased, so correct me if I am wrong. How do hormones and the changes they bring fit into your process?

JJ: I was emotionally unhappy and I didn't realise how emotionally at unrest I was until I started hormones. Physical changes are physical changes. As a trans person I welcome them but now emotionally I feel much more aligned. I love oestrogen. I feel blissful. I love waking up. It's not about beauty.

There's such an ease about you. You are conventionally and unconventionally beautiful, but there is such an ease. Everything about you is model-like. I imagine you'll have a great career in modelling.

JJ: I've been modelling now for half a decade. There is something so empowering now about being able to be an out trans model. I love that feeling on a catwalk, being openly me. There is something about being open and proud and stepping out onto a runway in Paris. It feels powerful, it is validation, but it is about my being trans and that space was unavailable to us before – we had to hide our transness.

I remember interviewing Caroline Cossey for an article about her wonderful career which was destroyed by being outed as a trans woman. She'd done cover after cover; she was an incredibly successful working model, denied the right to be out, proud and employed. It matters, it's life.

JJ: I have never had to deal with the before/after photographs. Andreja Pejic and Teddy Quinlivan are getting big campaigns now, being out and proud. It's our time. We are empowered to do it because it's almost presumed we can't break into the big time. I've walked shows in Paris and I felt in trans woman heaven. I was contacted by trans girls in countries where it is illegal, saying that it inspired them. I am a six foot one proud trans woman with no hips and a flat chest. I am so past ever thinking about shaving an Adam's apple.

Our spaces need to become 'usualised' to the point where they become comfortable. I imagine that being the only trans model would feel groundbreaking but also uncomfortable.

JJ: I don't feel like the token trans model that might be in others' minds when they employ me. I just want to do a good job.

Almost the objectivity in modelling allows people to think they can order us like that, but it's a job. I love modelling. As a trans woman my boyish body – flat chest, etc. – works for me. I enjoy it.

I think trans has an inherent value which is useful for breaking down body stereotypes which are often really damaging. Do genitals matter?

JJ: I've done runways in bikinis and stuff. It doesn't limit my career – that was my only worry. It does make it slightly harder to find a partner. It was annoying when I was single. I felt like I would have a boyfriend if I was cis and had a vagina because I'm tall, blonde, model-like. But I kept getting older guys fetishising me and objectifying me because of the perception of my trans body.

What word is it okay to use when we talk about your genitals?

JJ: Just 'genitals'. I'm not going to lie, I do have a degree of shame around. Only recently have I started to think about the space my genitals occupy in my life. I feel like it's the only category where I retreat. It's a painful space for me.

If someone were to draw an example of a beautiful, contemporary, edgy white model, they would draw you. I cannot imagine being 22, utterly desirable, but feeling this block.

JJ: I am so proud of being me, Josephine Jones. I just have experienced systemic prejudice and it pierced through me. It's about them and it got through my exteriority.

Did or does it feel like a dating deal-breaker?

JJ: For them, not me. I have had several instances where I've been on a few dates and we are now watching old movies and smoking spliffs in the bath, but then they realise I'm trans and it's over. I've had people say, 'My family wouldn't accept you and I'm left alone again. I feel like I have become the woman I need to be but I wonder if this will always get in the way. For them it is the deal-breaker.

Just to say that even if you have had the genital operation, the pussy op, it can still be an issue when we bump up to cis folk. It doesn't resolve their dysphoria.

JJ: My self-love and confidence almost allows me to get by that rejection.

Naively I did think the operation would save me, that somehow a neo-vagina would give me easy access to normativity – it didn't. I realised that nothing was added, just transformed. I was still being rejected just because I was trans. Some people even wanked off to my cave, but then when I told them it was a trans space the rejection happened. I watched people come watching me finger myself and then still deny it as a valid experience. That made me realise that I had work to do on owning my process totally and it meant owning and loving the cock and ball skin that lines my cave.

JJ: When people say, 'It's not for me', it's such a subjugation of everything that we are, our struggle, our journey, our authentic being.

Somehow, I feel we must feel or get comfort or peace in that process. How do you think you find, or will find, peace and comfort in fucking? Do you have a sense of ease now?

JJ: I feel like it's the one aspect where I haven't cultivated a confidence in my being. It makes me feel very vulnerable and fragile. I don't have the answers yet. I've made peace in not feeling angry about it. I'm a transgender high-fashion model. I refuse to add any more stuff to my list. I'm already an orphan.

I'm sorry if this questioning adds any fragility.

JJ: No, Juno, it's fine. I love your work but I'm not going to lie to you: I don't feel super comfortable talking about it, but I know it's important.

The vagina became so mythical in my mind that I assumed it would solve everything.

JJ: I don't think that one thing will be the thing that makes all the difference. It's no Indiana Jones quest. Maybe for a fleeting moment I bought into that.

But how do you date comfortably with that fragility? I know that naked my body is a trans body, I must somehow own its strength. I give myself credit now for having a great trans body, but it's taken years for me.

JJ: I think it's finding a way to move beyond that.

Being real on our own terms? Can we do that with the genitals of our choosing? Can we be robust in that respect?

JJ: I've had bad experiences that have made me feel fragile. It can feel that you are at the peril of your partner. It is almost just their decision. Candy Darling called it her 'flaw'. I'm still battling to see it not as a flaw. But rejections are hard to come back from. I find it hard to find intimate empowering experiences. If someone rejects me for, say, not being passable, I can think 'Fuck them, I've just done a spread in *Love Magazine* in Chanel haute couture', but there is something about the absoluteness of the rejection of your naked body that is hard to contend with.

Is coming, are orgasms, important to you?

JJ: I almost felt for a while that it would be enough for me to be with a guy who would accept me, and I would pleasure them, only very briefly.

I did that for years, sadly.

JJ: It's horrible. I only did it very briefly. I transitioned whilst in a relationship and he didn't dump me, but we still had a gay sex life with set dom/sub roles – quite binary in a way. But aside from that, when dating it felt like my cock and balls were literally standing between me and the kind of fictional contented relationship I could have. My friends would say that the right guy would come along and the wrong ones were dickheads whom I wouldn't want to be with. But even when I met guys who weren't dickheads, it still felt that it got in the way. Literally squished up in between us, ruining the relationship we could have.

It's such a pressure that idea of the 'right one coming along'. I just wanted to go online and be able to fuck and play without commitment to the 'right one'. It makes us often commit to anyone. I think we still must do so much work to make them feel comfortable and to couch our genitals. I spent years managing my genital area, pre- and after surgery. It stopped me having easy-breezy orgasms. If I meet someone online now and they ask about my genitals, I tell them I have upcycled, reconfigured cock and balls.

JJ: That's very brave.

It's my truth and I need to completely inhabit my truth and my body.

JJ: Sometimes guys fall in love with the fiction of you. With me they fall for the 'trans model' tag. Social media really doesn't help. Either way, it transcends surgery in the first instance. Trans femmes are so mythologised around sexuality. I'm not willing to slip easily into that bathtub of fetishisation.

It's important to just get down to our real bodies, our flesh, bone and skin.

JJ: I'm happy with self-performative objectification but not others doing it to us.

Often we negatively objectify our own bodies and genitals.

JJ: That's often informed by the partners and experiences we have. I still navigate that today. There's times I'm with my partner, whom I've been with for over a year, where I feel like I'm being pleasured and I'm happy, we're being intimate, but I can drop out and disassociate. I sometimes look away.

How does that stay as pleasure? Can you be touched there and come?

JJ: Yes, to both. I've always had orgasms. I always feel worthy of them. If a guy would have an orgasm and leave me, I would say. The fragility is more of an embarrassment. I know that I am worthy of pleasure. An orgasm for an orgasm.

Are our genitals gendered? You said you look away sometimes?

JJ: My partner Ruby makes me feel incredibly comfortable. They do a lot of work in allowing that comfort to happen.

[Ruby, Josephine's partner, comes in and sits down next to her on the large faded pink velvet sofa.]

Hi, Ruby. We were just talking about comfort and our bodies, and it really felt like Josephine was finding a comfortable space with you.

Ruby: We met just over a year ago in Berlin. There was lots of physical attraction.

JJ: Yes.

Ruby: And a lot of curiosity and lust. I think it's taken us a lot of time to learn about each other's bodies and boundaries and the different complicated needs we have.

JJ: We met across a crowded street in Berlin.

Ruby: You tell it so romantically.

Can you, just for simplicity and shorthand, describe yourself, Ruby?

Ruby: I'm a musician and artist. I have very complicated feelings about my gender and sexual identity. I see myself very much as being in a transitional state, but it's becoming clear that the transitional state is the state. I don't want to pin myself down. I generally present visibly in a gender variant way, although I don't really think that's a good way of describing that. I've always dated women and I hold onto the fact that I have been a male socialised person. I'm comfortable with that. It's been interesting to feel myself settle into a decidedly queer space and now a queer relationship.

Queer is useful shorthand for destinations.

JJ: I think I had always craved that normativity in terms of relationships, but the older I get the more I question that. Being in an unconventional relationship has meant almost mourning the loss of my conventional aspirations. To be honest, when we met I thought, 'Fantastic, a six foot five, androgynous boy.'

Ruby: I presented masculine when we met.

JJ: Thank god.

Ruby: It could have gone differently.

JJ: I thought I had met this tall, androgynous skater type, very feminine and fey, quiet, and I found that erotic. I still do, but now it's navigating that you are gender variant and genderqueer and that you always have been, and it's weird that for the first time ever my boundaries, my normative boundaries, are being challenged. There is a percentage of you that is neither masculine nor feminine. Are we quasi lesbian? I find it hard to not be in a simple heteronormative framework.

Perhaps if we reframed it as occupying comfort rather than strict labels and just experiencing feeling at ease.

Ruby: That's a really nice way of framing it.

I don't frame what's between my legs as upcycled because I want a radical label. Like others I want to be intimate, but I need to feel comfortable. That upcycled framing allows me comfort. It's about building a comfortable personal space – something as trans folk we are so often denied.

JJ: We are so emotionally comfortable with each other, our bodies and energy just clicked.

I can see that now. You both fit together and are so entwined. Did the sexual attraction remain through the changes you both encounter?

JJ: I had to renegotiate for a hot second and it wasn't even about you; it was about me feeling like I had to grieve the loss of being in a heteronormative relationship but at the same time what I loved about our relationship was its abnormality, I love that we both look like boys sometimes or that we are often both in dresses. I love our synergy.

Ruby: I like not having definitive cut-off points.

JJ: I like your ambiguity.

Ruby: I use 'they'/'them' pronouns and use 'Ruby' now so there is a definite difference.

JJ: It feels gradual. No one would be surprised if you went on to binary transition, but from everything you say it doesn't feel that's where you are heading.

Ruby: I just want to respect my future self. I can't make any definitive statements. I need to be in the 'right now'.

[At this point Ruby leaves the room and we stop for a glass of water.]

Partners really matter. After the first book it became clear to me that trans people in relationships with other trans people have a comfort that others often struggle to get, even in cis–cis relationships. It's about intimate comfort.

JJ: I still fight sexually to allow myself to exist in the safe space afforded to me by my partner because of the damage from previous relationships. There is this quote about Kate Moss where people say, 'She is a great model because she just takes her clothes off, she loves her body, she doesn't care.' I always found it annoying that I love my body, but there is this thing that means I walk around tucked in a bikini. I dream of finding the right photographer to shoot me naked. I don't view any of my body as male and feel ready to embrace comfort.

It's so important.

JJ: Venus with a penis. It's attached to me and I'm a woman, therefore respect it's a female thing. We need to move away from a coded non-language about our bodies.

Upcycled cock and balls rather than a vagina are my clarity.

JJ: Coded language is about safety.

It doesn't liberate though, and only through liberation will we truly find safety.

JJ: We almost learn to exist in discomfort. In tucking we find discomfort, and maybe it highlights a certain shame and pain that allows a different focus.

Is it painful?

JJ: It can be. Comfort is such a big deal. It allows empowerment. The discomfort is almost internalised as being a thing that trans women must endure. If I were to have genital surgery... I'm not planning it or on any list at present, but if I were, I think it would be a very physical thing to increase comfort, to remove that pain.

For me, the surgery allowed for congruence: cock and ball skin used to craft an internal space works well for me. It works for me, it's not a space centred on pleasing others.

JJ: I'd like to try and own the discomfort in my genitals. I think it's happening slowly, self-acceptance.

* * *

It's clear that so many of us spend years hiding our bodies, our genitals, our breasts and covering our nakedness whilst accepting pleasuring others and not ourselves. In seems for many of us that our concept of pleasure is derived from looking into another's eyes and seeing ourselves reflected within them. Their pleasure is somehow defining us as successful. Making them come allows us to access pleasure potential within our posited future selves and not within our actual bodies. I did that for many years, hiding my maleness under the covers or deep within clothes. I became great at sucking cock or being fucked in the arse, without any of my maleness being on show, being touched or needing attention. I accepted making myself come after they left or went out.

It's bleak to look back and see that my pleasure was always tinged and coloured by the effort it took to hide my presumed maleness. I never for a minute thought that a cock could be a female thing. Back then it was accepted set-thinking that if you were trans you would move along a linear path from one gender to another; there was no oscillation or interchangeability as there is growing now. I felt that all of my maleness (it's important for me now to own it) was dirty and had to be hidden away until the butterfly moment when I would emerge 100 per cent feminine. If ever I'd stopped to think rationally about the surgery, I would have realised far sooner that the demonised cock and balls would always be integral to my journey and, in binary terms, vital to my sense of womanhood.

The cock and balls actually make me woman in society's eyes.

That is a still a key premise we run from far too often when we are being attacked. We allow others to define gender as genitals, or gender as the shadow of past genitals.

The idea is that the cock is the problem and once it is gone we will be more acceptable as women. There is no data on the numbers of femme-defining trans folk worldwide who have 'gender realignment' surgery, but the costs, the lack of free healthcare (which includes gender realignment surgery) and the poverty that often accompanies trans people would lead anyone to reasonably assume that many of us will never, through choice or financial ability, be able to have surgery. Are we any less woman if we have a cock and balls, or any more woman if we have a neo-vagina crafted from cock and balls? It's exactly the same skin, components and vessels. In giving away the words 'vagina', 'woman' and 'real', I hope that I stop adding to the safety hierarchy that exists and celebrates us for all the wrong reasons. My cave is both female concept and male material, which nestles into trans destination neatly and beautifully. I own it, every last capillary and cell.

By saying this I am not demonising the process of surgery – I'd have it done again and again, it's my confirmation of my transness – but I am questioning how society views us and, worse, believes it owns us.

For me it's take-back time...

Taking back a largely ill-informed, misogynistic and paternalistic narrative that we are expected to exist within, and re-writing it ourselves without needing to perform and fight to gain access to the performance. The performance of gender.

The narrative written for us in order that 'they' can make sense of us is earth-shatteringly exhausting. We are currently little more than circus oddities jumping through hoops and being continuously judged and debated as spectacle. Even our greatest allies are still usually at arm's length.

Listening to Josephine talk about the discomfort of tucking, and how that exists as an everyday experience for many trans femmes and drag performers, seems to indicate an acceptance that the cock needs to be hidden for femme to work and be believable, and also that the penis can innately experience and handle pain and discomfort.

We have to talk about that in terms of its impact on how we are dividing up gender through a strict binary lens on our own bodies, quite possibly taking an entirely opposite position about gender as we're tucking. If we are saying that a penis can be a feminine/female thing, and a vagina can be a male/masculine thing, then we trap ourselves when we hide them. We verbally define them as free whilst we painfully and with great discomfort bind and tuck them away.

Obviously the pain of being misgendered and the pain of dysphoria often outweigh the discomfort and pain of hiding our bodies. It did for me, but at the very least we should start to discuss what it means to our sense of selves if our bodies and our genitals are allowed to be seen and experienced as part of us. The more we divide our bodies into acceptable and unacceptable, the more difficult it is for, say, a trans femme without surgery to ever go swimming in a public pool and feel beautiful, strong and safe. If we submit to the 'gender equals genitals' debate without reframing it in accordance with our own comfort as a baseline, then we will continue to endure pain and be bossed by all of those demanding we are one thing or not. Our reality is that we are born wonderfully congruent as trans beings; but in this current system, with its active punitive environment, we struggle to fit in and we struggle to become aligned within a system that still, almost universally, demonises women, sex, genitals, nudity, desire, desirability and intimacy. The system we are trying to fit into is not only deeply flawed but is also created from a religious perspective and base which would rather do away with any personal autonomy – look at the backlash in the United States against abortion. Our system sets out to destroy autonomy. It's a system that demeans and denigrates everyone apart from the men who look like the fictitious images of Christ. They get to try and fuck us all up, and not alone – many follow, many join in, many stand as silent bystanders.

As trans folk, we could and should be refusing to inhabit their painful demands and set about building our own communities in which we celebrate our bodies from the get-go – cocks and pussies and all. A space where we celebrate our transness as being unsullied by them. Fuck them and their toilet-panic. It's our spaces that get ruined by their submission to gender constructs and gender performance.

But even if the whole world issues a decree today that stated that trans women are women and trans men are men, then we trans folk will still have to align ourselves to our own inner truth that our bodies are trans bodies which we have the capacity and bravery to change, and that we encounter our bodies and ourselves as being fluid enough to make those changes. We will still have to find our freedom within the term 'trans' else we will be continuously chasing down the word 'real' until we exhaust ourselves in the attempt to be good enough for 'them'. We have to embrace our transness and be proud of its inherent truth.

The idea that we can actively own and control our processes, be they social or surgical or anywhere in between, is a new concept that challenges the structures that we exist in to change: to accept our transness as a reality that is as valid as any other. We can, if we completely embody our truths, push society to a point where gender norms don't function with the same weight, brevity or capital. But to do that we have to become much more robust and picky about the fights that so often drain our energy. The law says we can use the toilets we need to use. We don't have to fight for that, but we do have to take more legal action against those people who in attacking us are breaking the law. That works. We can never be victims of the current stupidity that is thrust against us, and they will only be victims of legal action because they are breaking the law. It has nothing to do with freedom of speech or shutting down debate.

A woman can have a penis – thousands do, there is no debate. A man can have a vagina – thousands do, there is no debate.

They are not a threat to you.

You are a threat to you with your obsessive reluctance to let go of gender stereotypes and gender constructs. I am a woman with a penis and balls reconfigured. I stand with my siblings.

I want us to ask the right questions, or better questions, around our surgery, not just the ones of 'looking real'. Questions like 'How does my cave grow and age?', 'How can I bring myself to orgasm?', 'Can someone fuck me hard without damage being done internally?', 'Is my cave robust enough for toys?', 'How often should I douche?' and 'Do I need follow-up appointments to check the scarring, etc.?' The list of good, empowering questions goes on and on.

These questions are becoming much more of a reality as younger trans folk are demanding surgery on their own terms, not simply as part of a medicalised process that is linear, sequential and hierarchical. I adore what both Josephine and Travis said about trying to work with their cocks. For them the alignment starts now with the bodies they have. It bodes well for self-care and growth. It bodes well for much younger trans folk who might already be considering a lifetime of stealth and hidden authenticity as being the safest way to exist.

We do our trans truth very well, we do their truth with fragility.

This debate always comes back to the question 'Can a woman have a cock?' Well, clearly in 2019 they can, and they can be utterly feminine with it. Both Travis and Josephine define as femme and both feel femme and both currently have cocks in cock configuration.

I started this chapter talking about April Ashley and her 'seemingly' heteronormative passage through surgery to define herself as a woman, seen as safe, as passing and beautiful.

Looking back, we see an apparent crowd-pleaser, but at the time she was as radical as you could be, fighting for life-risking surgery and then spending years being denied her authenticity as a woman, and still fighting up until after the introduction of the Gender Recognition Act 2004 when she could finally change her birth certificate.

To be trans and defined as a woman or man then was a radical act, a political act without the navel-gazing safety of an online forum or support group. Fuck knows how they made it through, but they did, and in the shadow of their legacy we must continue to redefine ourselves as we need. If that means keeping your cock and being woman, then so be it. If that means tucking and untucking in accordance with your own comfort, then so be it. If that means binding or not binding, having a phallosplasty or being fucked in your birth vagina and defining as resolutely masculine, then so be it. We owe April and all of our elders our commitment to fight to inhabit our bodies exactly as we want and not out of fear.

TYLER & FIONA

I'm exhausted travelling to my next interview.

I hate that being the opening line to this chapter, but you have to write the words you write. They're the only ones you have.

I've travelled by taxi, train, tube, plane, two further trains and another taxi, all crammed into a few hours of travel that started at 4 am and is taking me to the countryside, far away from London, to the North East, near to the beautiful city of Newcastle.

When I sit in the taxi on my last leg of the journey, I can feel the signs of exhaustion kicking in: the sores in my mouth, the thrush on my tongue, my head thumping, my body aching and my depression rising. So often in my life the depression takes over when I'm too tired to structurally push back against it by eating well, sleeping lots and taking the right kinds of exercise.

Sitting here in the back of the taxi, I just want to roll up into a ball, close my eyes and for some reason cry.

My depression has blighted my life, so often making me doubt my abilities, making me hide away, full of anxieties and panic. When it was really at its toughest, ten or fifteen years ago, I would hide away from the world, from people, from connections, from life. My house in Spain, deep in the mountains, is my sanctuary. My lifelong struggles with addiction have often served to hide my depression and anxiety. Opiate-based drugs dimmed and quietened the feelings of lost control and uncontrollable panic.

I don't like to talk about my depression, like I seldom talk about the impact of being HIV for many years, because both have been truly devastating, but through that devastation comes utter liberation. They are the cycles of my life, in which, somehow, I get much done. When I come out of a depressive period, it feels like the world around me is just full of potential, that I have potential. However old I have become, that feeling of newness after the dark never feels any different. On a day-by-day basis I adore sunrise and dread sunset. I'm always up early and I always go to bed early. I need to manage me in this way. It's part of the structure around my life that keeps me 'light' and not overwhelmed.

I wanted the opening of this chapter to be so different. I wanted it to be about journeys, distance and the changing landscape from South to North, but it's fast becoming a set of words, an admission, of my workable-isolation and the mental health struggles that have impacted so much of my life.

The taxi driver starts to tell me about the local area and how it was decimated by the pit closures but rescued by the car industry. This is a beautiful part of the world but tough and austere, not pretty. I've often thought in these confusing Brexit times that if I can no longer go between London and Spain then I will move to somewhere like this, rugged and remote from the South of England. The driver tells me it's about a thirty-minute journey, so I can relax. I try to relax, I close my eyes and think about the couple I am travelling to interview and then plummet into needing a hug, into trying to work out why I am not seeming to match up to what a hug needs. I blame me when I feel like this. I wish I fitted in more easily.

I open my eyes. Every day for the past twenty-five odd years I've opened my eyes and remembered being HIV positive. Then I thank every god and goddess that I'm still alive.

I don't talk a lot about being HIV to friends or family because they have lived through this with me and been terrified, especially in those early years, that I would die, but I get exhausted these days. It's actually exhausting not being able to speak about being exhausted and not being able to speak about the impact of having been HIV positive for around a quarter of a century, about the stigma and the isolation of being trans and HIV, the loss of simple intimacy.

In simple terms, my immune system has been fighting a fucker of a virus every day for the past twenty-five years or so. For many years now, brilliantly effective drugs have helped to fight the virus to the point where its effects are kept at bay, but when I get tired I struggle and always come crashing down. I have no mid-ground: I'm either whole or in pieces.

I keep telling myself that I cannot run from one end of the country to another and then run between Spain and London and back again. I need time to recoup and recharge, but the

AIDS voice which still lingers in my head tells me that sitting still means dying and that moving means being alive. It's a hangover from those early days, pre-treatment, when no matter how hard you tried to stay healthy and alive, most didn't. I lost so many close and dear friends that I still talk to in my head, all these years later. I have survivor guilt and survivor tenacity but also a survivor 'this is how you keep alive' mentality.

To get the plane at 7 am I had to get a taxi at 4 am and then a train at 4:15 am. I didn't sleep the night before because I was already overtired but also truly excited about this interview. The two people I'm travelling to see I only know through social media. I have consumed the online documentation of their struggles and their love story. I feel like a voyeur to their physical and emotional changes. I've been a witness, as many others have, to the blossoming of their relationship, so beautifully and powerfully shared that it pushed through online platforms with a raw intensity and honesty that made me want to write a second book in order to meet them.

They are my love story.

* * *

I'd seen both of you come together online through social media – Facebook and Instagram mainly. I became completely entranced by what felt like a beautiful love story. How did you meet?

Fiona: Well, it started off when Tyler randomly sent me a friend request online, I was really reluctant to accept his request because he didn't have any photos of himself. I get a bit put off if people just have random pictures but none of themselves. I need to know who I'm talking to. But for some reason I was drawn to him. Something was telling me to accept his request with good grace. We had mutual friends and it felt safe.

Tyler: We were both part of a trans group online. I was getting support from them offline, outside of the online group.

A local trans group?

Tyler: Yeah, based in Newcastle, a North East group. I'd reached out to the group for support because I couldn't get into Newcastle. They added me to the group online as well. I was just checking out who was in the group and I saw Fiona. I wasn't looking for anything but I instantly fancied her.

I get lots of requests from men in the American military who are looking for love and fun with the 'right lady'.

Fiona: Do you get those too? They always seem to be a captain or colonel.

Maybe they were a few years ago. So what happened after that? You have mobility issues that meant you couldn't get into Newcastle. Are you comfortable to talk about them?

Tyler: Yes. At the time when we first made contact online, I was bedbound. I'd just started my transition so I was just reaching out to make trans contacts. That's how I found the online group, but they met up in Newcastle. I was trying to find a way to make real contact with another person who was trans or a trans ally. It had to be someone who would come to me – it was such a barrier.

Being bedbound must have made it virtually impossible to connect with new people and start the process of transitioning?

[There is a real silence here. Tyler is visibly stressed. I've seen them online be so open and brave about their situation. I have no idea how tough this must have been. We allow the silence to wash around and over us.]

Tyler: It was so hard to get my head around how I was even going to start transitioning. I could hardly get my head round it. How would I access any service if I couldn't leave a single room? How would anyone take me seriously? How could I get them to come to me? How could I be visibly trans if I was in my bed? How could I be taken seriously in my own home? When I'm in bed, how do I get real-life experience that people take seriously? People cannot possibly understand being bedbound.

Do you mind saying how long you were bedbound for?

Tyler: No, it's fine. I was bedbound for three years, and before that I was housebound but just living in the one room. My bed was downstairs in the living room. I'd moved from the upstairs bedroom to try and be less isolated, but it didn't work out like that. I just shut the door. It was a total of about eight years housebound.

I've seen photographs of you both recently out and about.

Tyler: Yes. Last Saturday was the first time we've been on a night out together. It was like a first date.

Fiona: Every day we push the boundaries slightly further and further, seeing what we can do together.

Tyler: We help each other. But Fiona waited for two years to go out of the house with me. It was like working out a relationship but in one room. Fiona had her own place to start with – at the time you were working.

Fiona: I was constantly working for really low money.

Tyler: At that time we lived separately so Fiona had her own life outside of us.

The point you make about visibility is so important because most of the accepted ways that we prove that we are trans is to be outside.

Tyler: It's constantly like that for me. I'm always trying to prove who I am.

I think you are taken seriously by an awful lot of people in your social media feeds; by a lot of people that matter. I came here by taxi, train, tube, plane, two further trains and another taxi, because I take you, both of you, your relationship and your online work really seriously.

Tyler: I think the validation I get online really matters. It helps me have that in myself. But the medical route needs something different from me, from us. Trying to prove that I want to be outside the house and am not choosing to stay in is really diffi-cult... As if I just want to be in here by myself.

Fiona: You still feel that you have to prove stuff to them. I take photographs whenever we go out.

Tyler: And I don't like it all the time. I don't want photographs taken just for them.

But surely they know and accept why you can't go outside?

Fiona: I'll answer this, if that's okay? [*Looks at Tyler.*] The NHS does recognise Tyler's condition but they have said that to pro-gress with surgery he needs to not be having the dissociative seizures. It's virtually impossible to go out without becoming stressed and having one.

Tyler: My seizures are caused by dissociation. I originally had ME that really progressed and got much worse. It started when I was around eighteen, but it wasn't diagnosed for years. The seizures got much worse when I was bedbound. They became 24/7. I think that people just see it as depression. At my worst I couldn't bear any sound, or noise or situations I wasn't comfortable in. I would have seizures continually. I got used to functioning and having symptoms. People said my case was extreme. I think I've got a lot better now and don't have anywhere near as many symptoms.

Fiona: No, you've really progressed and can do a lot more of your day-to-day stuff. You can sit and hold a conversation for quite a long time now without symptoms. A few months ago this wouldn't have happened.

I feel incredibly honoured to be let into your space. How did you connect with the gender services?

Tyler: I did have a limited amount of appointments from the gender clinic where they would visit me at home. I really had to fight for them. I waited so long they had to have an independent assessment just to get them to come out to the house. Understandably it takes more time to come and see me. They had to allocate a few hours to me when they could be seeing more people.

But how many people are there with your complex needs? You should just be seen. How easy is it for you to get out now?

Tyler: This house really helps – it's all open plan. When Fiona found the house, the fact that it didn't have doors and that my room could be downstairs and in the middle of everything was really important. It's really helped.

What was it like for you, Fiona, when you met Tyler back when he was still bed- or room-bound? How did your relationship happen and grow to the point where now you are living together in your own place?

Fiona: The first time I came to visit Tyler, your mum came to pick me up from the train station. I was as nervous as hell, I get real anxiety around new people.

Tyler: It was so weird to meet a new person but have to send your mam to get them.

Fiona: I'm not going to lie, it did feel bizarre and very strange, especially when I was greeted by two big dogs jumping up and going mad at me – not aggressive or anything, but just excited. And then going down a corridor to your room, which would have been the living room. The door was shut. I had no idea what to expect.

Tyler: I was used to the dark, so I still had my curtains drawn. I always had the curtains shut.

Fiona: I believe your curtains were open a little bit and there was a little bit of light coming in.

Tyler: I would have done that for you.

Fiona: It was such a nerve-wracking day.

What a first date!

Tyler: That's why I kept putting it off. Fiona wanted to meet, but I kept postponing.

Fiona: It was such a beautiful thing. Every time I came home from work, there would always be a comment from Tyler on my posts. He never sent me direct messages. I would come straight in from work and see if you had left a message for me. It was a really nice way to communicate. It felt leisurely and relaxed.

It was always about a topic, so there was no awkwardness. I found it easy. It went on like that for at least a month. We met up on the 19th January.

Tyler: She knows the exact date!

So you meet up, you open the curtains a little bit to let the light in for Fiona. I have to say I feel completely honoured to be in your space, interviewing both of you. It must be a big deal to have me in here?

Fiona: It think it's soothing to be able to talk to you in here about this stuff.

Tyler: You probably haven't had a chance to talk about it.

Fiona: It's nice to talk to someone else.

You must be spending lots of time together inside. I can see why it's been so important for you both to build the large online communities.

Tyler: I was putting a lot of effort into building and maintaining something outside of here. Keeping some of me outside really matters. It's a bit of a fear now that I could go back to being housebound. I don't think I ever would, because I'm in a different headspace. I have to have something outside. It's not for validation but to see me outside of here, knowing I'm getting better.

Can we go back in time to that first date on the 19th January?

Fiona: I found it weird arriving through the back of the house, like Tyler was the president, me picked up in a big black car and then coming in the back way. The door was closed and I didn't know if by opening it I would be breeching their privacy.

Tyler: I was aware of all of this. You can't help it when you're in that situation and you are bringing someone into your small world. I was really afraid of that. It wasn't like I just had health barriers that you can cover up or make invisible until you both feel comfortable and then talk about them. It was there. My vulnerability was there immediately. I was in bed. I had to ask Fiona to leave the room if I needed to go to the loo. Fiona had to sit on the bed. It didn't feel appropriate – I'm dead proper and it didn't feel right for a first date. We're both sitting on the bed.

Fiona: I didn't know what to say at first. I was thinking, 'Talk about anything.'

Tyler: We're both quite shy.

Fiona: I was thinking, 'Pick a random subject.' If it was relevant or not, I had to say something.

Tyler: Before we met we both had the same barriers, so we'd never spoken on the phone. We were both scared what the other would think about our voice.

Fiona: I'd just started hormones and my voice was so deep. I still don't like it, but I'm not bothered about trying to change it now.

Tyler: But that's why we never talked on the phone. I wanted to come across in a certain way and I was worried I wouldn't. We would leave each other short videos – that felt different. You'd leave me a video message on a night time, so I had one to wake up to in the morning. So we had kind of got used to each other.

So you both had all of those fears that often happen when we start to transition but you also had all of your other fears around being in the one room. What made it, or how did it, move on from that first date?

Fiona: I just thought from day one, here's an incredibly handsome, brave guy who's put himself out there to see me. I was really drawn to him. I thought he was really interesting.

For you there was never any question: you saw the essence of Tyler straightaway?

Fiona: Yes, it's never happened before to me ever. I tell Tyler every day what a great relationship this is. I know I'm in the right relationship. I feel so comfortable and happy.

Tyler: It felt like 'This is the one?'

Fiona: I feel so safe with Tyler. It's hard to describe. Every day I wake up next to him and smile. It's magical.

It must be such a lovely thing to know that you are making another person so happy and so safe?

Tyler: She always tells me how happy she is. I think the things that we both needed we find in each other. Making Fiona feel

safe is important to me. Fiona likes the idea of a more traditional relationship, whereas I was open and didn't have many
expectations.

Fiona: Since living with Tyler I've got a real sense of security.
When I lived on my own, I felt vulnerable and I would lock
my doors.

Tyler: Until we moved here, you didn't feel that security.

Fiona: I had quite an insecure childhood and past, where I'd
moved around a lot. This is the first time I've had a sense of
stability. Tyler makes me feel really secure. I feel like I can let
my hair down now.

*When did your relationship move to being physically intimate, do
you mind me asking?*

Tyler: I know when. I just want to see if Fiona remembers.

Fiona: It went in stages, to be honest.

Tyler: It was about six months in.

Fiona: Do you want to answer this one then, as you remember?

Tyler: It just stuck with me.

Fiona: Actually, it went from not being physical to being really
physical.

Tyler: It was still dependent on my health though. There were times where I would have to think about what I was able to do. At that point I was still bedbound. My headspace was still in that kind of bed: the kind that you can't get out of, and not the kind you have sex in. It felt like the least sexual place to me. It felt like a caring environment.

This feels incredibly sexual now and like a beautiful love story. Not a hint of clinical caring, just love and caring from a loving place.

Tyler: I think I was so used to that clinical setting though that it took me a long time to get out of that. So, I was worried in the early stages that I might repeat that kind of caring role, but I was determined for it not to be about that. I wanted it to be sexual.

There was a lot going on around that bed: early transitioning, getting to know someone new in quite tough circumstances, becoming un-bedbound. It must have been tough for that space to actually adapt or change?

Tyler: It was a single bed, by the way, so even the size of the bed felt like a barrier. Are you really going to invite someone to be sexual with you in a small single bed?

Did it happen then and there, or were you living together before the barriers really came down?

Tyler: Fiona started to come over more and more, and stay over more and more.

Fiona: I think I slowly moved in.

Tyler: You still kept your flat for security?

Fiona: Yes, in case anything went wrong between us, I couldn't be homeless. Until we actually got this place here together, then I let it go.

Tyler: We talked a lot about the dysphoria that we felt. We talked about the areas of our bodies that made us feel dysphoric and were out of bounds. Gradually, though, everywhere has become less out of bounds. I think I had more boundaries – not just to do with health but body boundaries, upper and lower. I think at the time Fiona was like, 'Well where can I touch?' She couldn't get much physical contact because I'd get freaked out.

What was that like?

Fiona: At first it was like, 'Okay, I respect your decision' and I loved being with you, spending time with you.

Tyler: But did it feel at all sexual for you?

Fiona: I still felt really close to you and it was easy to wait.

Tyler: I could touch Fiona.

Fiona: I still had boundaries about the lower part of my body.

Tyler: But I could still make it about you, the experience. I had so many boundaries still.

Fiona: It was only the top half of me that I was happy to be touched.

Tyler: It was limited.

Did the limits start to go?

[*They both laugh.*]

Fiona: Yes, we are way past limits now. When we moved here, new bed – our own bed – things became much easier and progressed to where there are not really limits anymore.

Tyler: We talk about things a lot and are always re-assessing what each other's boundaries are.

Fiona: We do have planned intimacies, where we will say if we feel alright physically, 'Let's have a quick one later.'

Tyler: It's never quick. But if we are going to, then I need to rest, so in a way it has to be planned. I'm exaggerating a bit, but it is a little like that.

Fiona: It does help us both if we know when we are going to get physical. It helps me to know when things might happen. I like being prepared.

[*The laughter from both of them is infectious.*]

Tyler: You don't like things being sprung on you, do you?

The level of care and consideration you have for each other is beautiful. Watching you both from here, all I can see is this physical interchange of support. As one might be struggling, the other moves forward to touch or to take over. The interplay, consideration and the shared sense of consent you have is amazing and I'm not sure I've ever witnessed it to this degree.

Fiona: For us this bond is about having had really bad times before we knew each other and then meeting this person that you are completely in tune with, that understands when you need support or space. We know each other's mental states by just looking at each other. We just know.

Tyler: When we met we were in a similar space transition-wise. We were at the same point. As we got more freedom in ourselves, then it allowed us to be more at ease with each other. It really helped, so whatever other problems or barriers we faced we were at the same point in relation to our trans journeys. That made it much easier.

Fiona: I'd already started hormones about a year before meeting Tyler, but the levels were all over the place. They sorted it out about four months before meeting Tyler.

Tyler: We were both used to spending time alone, being quite isolated.

Fiona: I was isolated as I lost lots of friendships when I transitioned.

It's such brilliant fate that the two of you found each other.

Tyler: I'd completely ruled out ever having a relationship at the time, but something in me really reached out to her, even though I accepted being celibate.

Is this the perfect relationship?

Fiona: For me, yeah. I love everything about our relationship, from the physical and sexual stuff to the time we spend talking. Just being with each other is magical: having a hot chocolate on an evening together, talking about our days. Even if we are in the same house, we do completely separate things. In the evenings we sit down here and chat, just the two of us and the dog.

Tyler: The more I can do physically, the more I can just get on with my life, letting Fiona get on with hers independently. I can now go into the kitchen and the bathroom. I can make drinks and just get on. I work out every day. Walking is still difficult, but I don't use the wheelchair in the house, just outside.

Fiona: When I started transitioning, I didn't think anyone would want me and then Tyler came along and all this happened. I still think every day how lucky am I. It almost brings a tear to me eye that I found someone as loving as Tyler, who has opened his heart up to me. I get lost for words when I try to explain it.

You've explained it beautifully. What's the future?

Fiona: We'd love to get married.

Tyler: Fiona likes all the traditional stuff. It matters to her, her ideal picture. If it works for her, it works for me. It's security. Validating and making Fiona feel secure matters to me. I'm always bothered about how she is and how she is feeling. I'm not interested in what anyone else feels about us. I'm not looking for them to validate us. I'm not performing for anyone.

It doesn't feel like there is any performance. Your relationship feels far more sophisticated than that.

Tyler: The first time we were intimate together I had a real meltdown, I got so stressed with dysphoria that I had a night of vocal seizures and stuff. Was it the whole night?

Fiona: Yes, it was really difficult because I thought what had I done wrong, was he okay?

Tyler: I had to relearn how to feel. I had to relearn actually having orgasms. I learnt with Fiona.

Fiona: I'm so comfortable with Tyler, physically and mentally. I have let go of all my boundaries. I have learnt how to have sex with Tyler with my complete body. Every time we have sex now, we discover new things to try and do. When we are intimate I don't have dysphoria anymore. I am too interested in enjoying the moment and feeling pleasure.

Tyler: I don't experience it anymore either. I've built up my confidence now.

Fiona: I think we have taught each other that we are okay.

* * *

Sorry for talking about my HIV and my depression. It feels like I've co-opted the start of this chapter to talk about something way out of the remit of this book. I have an idea in my mind of the stuff I will say and should say.

As someone still struggling to have simple easy-breezy sex, I feel like I have a responsibility to write 'happy'. Who wants to get down and dirty with a person at an age when they should be 'sorted' and 'resolved'? In these times of endless attacks on our community, I feel like I should be ruthlessly positive and not add any other layers for those people seeking to do us harm to crawl into and shout out, 'See, they were unbalanced all along.' As someone who struggles with mental health issues, I keep quiet about them for that very reason: 'Working-class, ex-drug-addict who struggles with depression... That's why they call their neo-vagina an "upcycled cock and balls"... Because they're unhinged.'

I'm not, and I know exactly why I'm saying the things I say. It's because I simply want to create new, fresh, unsullied space in which we can move and breathe easily. Just a sliver.

That's the stigma of mental health and HIV though. So insidious are they that I feel like apologising for myself. I write about everything from colouring-in my old cock and balls to the new configuration of them, but somehow my HIV and my depression still have the capacity to make me feel like I might be judged, because my life tells me that I will be (hopefully not here though – my book feels like a safe space).

But even as I wrote the opening, I thought, 'How unsexy of you, Juno, to spill them old HIV and depression beans. No wonder no one wants to kiss you.'

After the interview, in the taxi on the way back to the local train station, I feel numb. I don't know why, but there is an awful lot to process. I have the same taxi driver on the way back to the station as on the way here. That feels reassuring. Small things can really make a huge difference. Like a person leaving comments on a Facebook post for someone to read when they come in from work – a small indirect gesture that led to Tyler and Fiona finding each other and coming together through the most extraordinary and challenging circumstances. Both trans and love have found a way. It was beautiful to hear and see how symbiotic their relationship is, but on many other levels it wasn't simply a straightforward love story that was easy to record and hear. It was visceral and tough.

At times I felt intrusive, clumsy, and at times I said, 'We can stop if you need to.' They never wanted to. Their generosity was mind-blowing. I felt it was such an honour for me and felt huge respect for them for allowing me into their space and their lives.

The issue of being seen, being visible, doing the whole 'real-life test' in whatever formal or informal sense it is now, is severely challenged by being at first bedbound and then housebound. How do you prove to the world that you exist with authenticity when no one sees you and you cannot be named, read, formed or received in the eyes of others? There is no gaze – or rather for at least three years there was only minimal contact with the outside world – so you are becoming authentic but only you can judge how that feels and looks, and how you might fit into the world with your new sense of authenticity and selfhood. The only naming and renaming is done by you, perhaps in the reflection of your online activity or perhaps reflected in a mirror.

Somehow Tyler had the strength and belief in themselves to reach out. What a small but fucking epic move.

When people question transness, they should think about Tyler's transness finding a way to exist, to breathe and to be seen. At the same time, Fiona's courage and determination to connect, and her belief in all things good – in love, companionship and human connections – allowed her to continue walking down that corridor and into that darkened room on their first date. Such commitment to being alive and finding happiness is a remarkable testament to our strength as trans folk. So often we focus on our fragility, yet across this world of ours trans folk pepper their days, their weeks, their lives with such optimism that they can make things be alright.

Epic.

Trans is epic, trans is belief in being alive and making life better.

Trans is life itself. It exists without being seen, it exists in the dark, in the womb, without language. It always did and it always will.

It is light and dark and all the gradations in between. It doesn't need labelling, fighting for, justifying, politicising or policing. It just is. We just are.

It can exist in a bed alone and it can grow, mature and refine itself by itself for itself. Trans doesn't need a reflection.

The taxi drops me by the station in Newcastle. For some reason I don't get the first train but go into the town centre to see if Waterstones has my first book, *Queer Sex*, in store. For some reason I want to photograph it. I'm feeling insecure and fragile and I need to touch base with myself, and I think that holding my book might ground me.

It's been a tough, long day and my body aches.

Somehow the strength that is both abundant and epic in Tyler and Fiona's relationship makes me realise my own fragility. I'm so often alone writing in isolation that it's like I don't really believe I exist. I'm alone so often that I need reflective feedback. It's a form of validation and vanity. I think I need a person in my life, but for now my book might do.

MICHAEL
& ME

*I thought someone would teach me how to paint a landscape, but
I never found that person so I just had to settle down and try.*

Georgia O'Keeffe

This beautiful summer's morning we've woken in a cavernous hotel room in Manchester, the hotel we couldn't find for ages despite using two different versions of Google Maps on each of our phones. We still couldn't find the hotel, even when the maps were saying 'You are at your destination.' Somehow, we stood staring at a car park, both of us wondering, 'Is this it?' and neither turning to see the huge, quite smart hotel behind us. Age is a wonderful thing.

I look over at Michael sleeping, their eyes covered with an eye mask which looks like a proper one that would completely shut out the light, not the kind the man in *Fifty Shades* brings out for their kink games, which are just really versions of naughty fluffy hand-cuffs and vanilla fuckery. What a strange film – like a sleek, slick version of a *Carry On... Carry On Getting Kinky*. Naughty sex is always the place society goes to prove that it is still vibrant. In my strangely convoluted mind I saw the first film and thought, 'Oh well, the end of days.'

I look at Michael sleeping. Actually, with all the sleep paraphernalia they are wearing they could be wide awake. I can just see an ear-plug peeking out of their ear. It looks like a bright yellow worm snaking out. I'm obsessed with their sleeping paraphernalia. It feels proper and prepared. Rightly, somehow they must have known that I don't sleep well, that I have bouts of insomnia. Maybe I've told them before?

They've come prepared to shut out the noise and the light and maybe my incessant need to talk.

People have always told me I talk too much. Michael never has, but the sleeping gear perhaps tells a different story. I love the frankness in the way they live their life. They are utterly committed to being in the moment.

It feels strange to be in a shared room, sleeping with someone, even if in separate beds. It feels like intimacy, like stealing their chips did last night. I wonder what it would be like to be in the same bed. I was always quite uncomfortable sharing a bed for a whole night. I love my own space. I've grown accustomed to being in a bedroom alone. I like it.

I love curling, uncurling, stretching out and wrapping all of the cover around me or throwing the whole thing off. I love my two dogs climbing up on the end of the bed in the morning when I have a cup of tea. I've had two dogs for years now – never one, always two and they are always very spoiled.

I never have been great at sharing this kind of close, intimate space. I would adore a partner but I'd like them to have their own bed, maybe their own bedroom, maybe their own house, maybe in a different town or country. It's no surprise that I'm single.

I've never said that before, not aloud. I'm almost embarrassed by it but I'm not sure why.

It's always felt like it was something I should be ashamed of. I love sex, I love affection, I love the physicality of another but I don't love or need that to be demonstrated daily by their being right next to me. I love elaborating and twisting conversations much more than hugging through a whole night. I love S&M games but I don't need a full-time S&M lover or a playroom in my house, where there could instead be art materials and books. It feels like too much of a thing, a static thing, sharing a bed every night with the same body. I feel contrary. I love starting a new book or a new article.

I remember visiting older relatives when I was a kid and finding out (it always seemed to be a shameful, hidden secret) that the couple slept separately. To me it always seemed like a smart choice. As kids, in a relatively small house, we had to share a room. The thought of having to share a bed with someone every night always felt constrictive and somehow suffocating. Having separate beds always felt like an utterly tender act in which a relationship could exist beyond intimate proximity. Having to share a bed every night with the same person just felt like a false commitment to intimacy as being a thing that only exists in close proximity. Maybe that's an excuse, maybe not.

It's a little like being monogamous though. I always struggle with the idea that a human should only commit to me and I to them. When I had relationships, when I was younger, people would often say to me, 'Aren't you at all jealous?'

I wondered, 'Jealous of what? You flirting?' It seems healthy and kind of sexy to watch you flirt. You coming in and telling me you have fucked with someone else again seems healthy and kind of sexy. I'm only troubled by the stuff you feel you have to tell as opposed to the stuff that remains silent. Us not talking anymore, us not discussing the important stuff anymore – politics, philosophy and art – that I'd miss, that I have a real sense of loss over, maybe even betrayal.

I dislike the idea that another person would need to get everything from me in order to make their world go round. What a pointless responsibility.

I knew that I needed more than that. To me the important intimate things were the things we shared that weren't physical: our artistic endeavours, our opinions, our intellectual and critical hikes through books, landscapes and works of art. It made me feel like a freak that I couldn't enact jealously to confirm a relationship. But I couldn't. I refused to waste that energy. I've never met anyone that could share that distant intimacy with me. Being trans and being HIV positive only added different layers to that sense of disconnection.

Knowing Michael has, for some cosmic reason, given me the strength to say this stuff aloud. Our friendship is partly based on the comfort we feel between each other to live and exist authentically and perhaps intimately without needing for it to grow towards physicality. I did think at one point that we might fuck in some way or another, and I feel sad that we haven't because that never fitted. It's indescribable as to why it didn't fit but it's a real fact about us to the point that where I lie and watch them sleep it's like watching a film. I wish they'd wake up so we can chat over breakfast.

* * *

Do you think that trans always needs to be witnessed in order to exist?

Michael: I think as humans we always need to be witnessed.

Why?

Michael: I guess I think that because we are all in social, cultural contexts, aren't we? And there is this old idea of being mirrored back, or getting affirmed, whatever identity it is we have landed in.
[*Long pause.*] It's not always affirmed either. It's often challenged.

What's the 'five days post-surgery picture all about'? Who is going to affirm, or is it just about being seen? I've literally seen trans women filming the packing coming out and posting it online. What's the get-back?

Michael: I think it's the idea of naming and renaming. We have talked about this a lot. If I am putting something out there about myself, that is a very specific gendered thing and if that gets fed back in a positive way then in a sense my gender is affirmed: 'Look, I've got this bicep' or 'Look, I've got this' (whatever it is).

I want to talk about genitals in a bit but I wonder what is our start-point? Is it a concept or a feeling, and where is the naming or renaming being added to? It sometimes feels like trans confidence can easily evaporate or be triggered to evaporate, so the naming and renaming doesn't seem to develop robust structures?

Michael: I'm not sure I understand. Is that a question?

Yes, but let me put it like this: Is the renaming done so that we can move through that day, or is the renaming done so that an idea of the self is fully formed - a long-term aim and at one point we don't need the affirmation of renaming?

Michael: No, I think it needs to be perpetual to give the illusion of a stable, secure identity.

And everyone does that, it's not just us?

Michael: Yes, I think so. We all did it before coming out as trans.

In crude terms, because we sometimes change our genitals, our start-point is what and where? It's like we build from the ground up, like growing a cock inch by inch. I disavow the word 'vagina', or give away that word because for me it doesn't fit. It leaves me without a word and therefore it can't be renamed. I don't think there is a word yet for the surgery that occurred. For me, I see it as trans affirming and not gender realigning and therefore the outcome is upcycling or reconfiguring but not replacement with a vagina. I see it as being a trans space. I'm struggling with the discomfort of not being able to easily rename.

So how does that become a workable renaming process? It feels bleak.

Michael: Why? The renaming and naming has to happen because there is no original, so renaming has to happen perpetually. You're not doing that. Isn't that more exciting?

I'm grappling with it because it is uncomfortable. I always had a very binary, linear idea of what my journey would be. That's still largely the empirical acceptance of us, especially from a broad range of allies who rename constantly, i.e. trans women are women; trans men are men. It feels uncomfortable to be out of that renaming loop-ease. That reductive and simplistic voice overrides almost everything else with the occasional caveat of 'don't forget nonbinary', as if that can occupy all the space between and around the binaries. All that space renamed as 'nonbinary', rather than 'trans', like a huge dredging net.

But I exist in this binary world and I am having to try to name myself in relation to it – for comfort, if nothing else. I'm not trying to be awkward. I would use 'vagina' if it felt right for me. 'Vagina' has lots of connotations, meanings and societal norms that mine doesn't have.

Michael: Such as?

For example, its structure is different: the skin, it's crafted out of some cock skin and some scrotal skin and then stitched together. I want to know how will that age, how robust is it? These are trans specific questions. I feel like if the naming is wrong, then what follows on will be wrong. I want more clarity for us so that, for example, we can own our holistic healthcare needs.

Michael: So, for you, if the word 'vagina' is used, then all the assumptions about cis vaginas are also used, which for you isn't the case.

For some people that might feel real enough or present enough but for me it isn't. I still have to perform my way into a cis-vaginal space.

Michael: But when you are talking purely anatomically, for you it isn't your truth?

No, it was sewn together out of a cock and balls. It's a different space. I'm tired of performing. From its inception it is a different space. Externally it might look exactly like a vagina, but everything else is different. But no one knows about them – trans vaginas, or 'transginas' as the wonderful Kate OD would say, are a great mystery to most, because for renaming sake it helps us to occupy the 'looks real' trading post.

If we need vaginal care, most of the time it is suggested to us that we return to the gender place in which they were given life, because gynaecological doctors run for the hills screaming, 'Never seen one of those before.' It's not good enough. It doesn't promote safety or good health.

But my lack of ability to easily name and rename makes me feel lonely. It's a cathartic employment, it's human. Me saying 'I'm trans, I'm trans' feels quite lonely. There aren't enough of us for that naming to reverberate and create a renaming energy.

I think some of the stuff that you've said makes me feel that you feel a bit like that?

Michael: I think, maybe. I mean I use the word 'dick' (don't I?)

as I understand my body, so I do use that term, even though I've never had a phallosplasty and don't intend to.

Isn't your use of the word 'dick' more about dick energy?

Michael: I don't think it's a different understanding. I think my use of the word is fairly standard.

So it's just like any other thrusting cock?

Michael: [*Laughs.*] Yes, more or less. But now it's more complicated because I'm on T and my own physiological body is changing, my own genitals that I grew are changing. I now have two concepts of dick: one is the one I talked about in your other book, which is the dick that I purchased.

How do you purchase a meaningful dick?

Michael: Just realistic, expensive and realistic.

[*I laugh.*] *When you say 'realistic', do you get them made to match you?*

Michael: No, I haven't got that much money.

[*We both laugh.*]

Michael: I heard there is a workshop and people carve their own cocks.

Out of what?

Michael: Out of wood. My dad was a stonemason and very crafty, but I still don't think any carved dick I made would look anything like the real thing. Maybe like a courgette.

So when you rename, what are you renaming?

Michael: Well, I'm renaming the word 'dick' and I use the term 'masculine'. But I don't think that I do a lot of renaming in the world. I just feel inside my essence is masculine, but I don't think I do much naming in the world. I might say my pronoun is not 'she' but that's about as far as my renaming or naming goes.

So why don't you?

Michael: Because what's the point?

But that's my point. That's the nub of it for me. I hate patriarchy, misogyny and sexism. I've seen and experienced the damage of all of it. I have no desire to rename my way into all of that but I do have a desire to name and rename my way into trans. I think renaming is a way of honouring that destination that you have reverence for or towards. No one renames, I don't think, negatively.

Michael: I also like the word 'trans'.

It's so unfettered and uncluttered. We have allowed the cis world to inhabit it and fill it with stuff, feeling sorry for us or angry towards us or saying that we're bad. It's actually an open and spacious word, without a lot of set meanings. If someone was going to describe 'trans', they'd probably start using anti-terms: 'wrong body', 'unhappy', 'suicidal'. I want to rename from a positive start-point.

I think the way you talk about your dick is entirely positive.

Do you think your naming is in a process with your dickage? Do you see your naming going to a different start-point? If, because of T, your body grew a marvellous dick, which would need more consistent renaming: the grown or the purchased?

Michael: Neither. So far everything on T feels very congruent. The dick on my body feels as congruent as the dick I bought. Nothing feels new or odd. It all sits in the same corner of the room in my mind. This is how I relate to my erotic identity.

Sex is the biggie for you. I cannot imagine you allowing any of your process to detach you from sex in anyway?

Michael: So much of my gender identity is to do with my sexuality, sexual arousal and sexuality.

It's very nice talking over orange juice and croissants. You talked a while ago about wanking with your grown dick. Do you feel comfortable talking about that over breakfast?

Michael: Yes, fine. I'm happy to talk about it.

It's really useful to hear about your process. In the first book you talked so beautifully about grown and non-grown.

Michael: So as a result of taking the T, my dick has grown, is growing. So now when I self-pleasure I also use my grown dick as part of my wanking, the only difference being...

[*Long pause.*] So on an imaginable level the two dicks are identical. There's the physiological dick and the dick I purchased. But on a physiological level there is a difference because I have nerve endings in one.

Are they joined together? If you were to wank with your hand, is there one motion?

Michael: On my literal body?

Do your two dicks attach or are they separate?

Michael: No, they're not separate at all. When I'm getting aroused, the notion of my dick – the notional dick, so to speak – is what is turning me on.

That's such a fluidity to your thinking. You push my space and thinking to think about essence much more.

Michael: I feel my essence, deep inside, underneath all the layers of however society sees me and however I might present in the world. Strip away all of those layers and my core is masculine. I can't say that it's nonbinary or gender neutral. I can't say it is agender. For me, my truth, my very core, is masculine.

But what does that mean? you're putting it forward as being an authentic essence, so what does that look like as opposed to performed masculinity? I don't think you are great at doing performed masculinity, but what for you is the distinction, if there is one?

Michael: I would say that the felt sense, a knowledge, without understanding how I got the knowledge. It's not like I'm masculine because of any behaviours. I know that I am masculine without knowing how I know. I just don't know what else I could call it without sounding too mystical.

Do you know how to perform an innate sense of self? Often when we perform, we are performing cis and performing the patriarchy. I wonder what your YouTube video would be like?

Michael: I'd say I'm performing with myself. Part of it could be fantasy, part of it could be reality. I went to the endocrinologist recently and he asked me a number of things: 'Have you noticed anything about your genitals? Your body hair?' That's the first person that's ever asked me anything like that or commented, but internally I'm monitoring myself rather than performing. I don't think I'm getting more facial hair, because I've always had loads, but certainly the genitals are changing. It's more of a feeling. In a way it's a little like my proprioceptive sense is moving closer, which sounds obvious. I'm not conscious of huge changes. I haven't had any work done that requires validation.

Is validation important to you?

Michael: Not really, no. Invalidation is important.

Invalidation is like misgendering – simply violence. It's like some-body getting something wrong again and again is an act of violence – maybe careless violence but felt as violence all the same.

185

Michael: Validation has never been that important to me. I used to live in a household full of trans men back in the 90s and somebody said was I going to transition and I said no because I already felt like I was male. Like I've said to you before, I could wear a dress (not that I want to), but it doesn't take away anything from my essence. Apart from someone saying 'woman'/'she', which is horrible, I don't need someone to go, 'mate, mate' repetitively to 'mate' me. I don't need that kind of affirmation.

I think until we get to a space where we are not naming and renaming using their cis-centric terms alone, then we are always relying on legalese or the kindness of strangers for our robustness and community structures. We are aiming for normativity because it's a numbers game. That's a truism that we employ but which doesn't ever encompass us. It's about structures that they police. They police themselves, let alone us. Us coming along with our reconfigured bodies and hormonal streams are almost beyond their ability to police, so they attack us, often violently. It's almost the Stockholm syndrome, with us continually trying to both mirror them and imbue excessive amounts of sympathy from them towards us, as we proffer our suicide statistics and victimhood. I think Butler might say that we become ungrieveable whilst we are still present. I think in trying to emulate and elicit empathy from them we all but disappear. Many might be entirely (and justifiably) happy with that, but for me it's inauthentic, reductive and aims to please a broken model.

I think in a hundred years' time we are going to be in an entirely different place, because it feels like younger people – younger trans people – need far less stereotypical naming. We think we are quite boringly currently obeying all the unwritten laws of patriarchy.

I think breaking away will allow us to be a lot less indebted to them and our position will be away from patriarchal paternalism.

Michael: Hopefully in a hundred years' time the notion of male and female will be a lot less rigid, because that's the essence of the problem: the two points which everyone else has to place themselves in relation to, even nonbinary. We are the change, or like Travis says, 'We are the gift.' By our very being in the world, we have the capacity to shatter that rigidity.

One of the things I was interested to talk about was the join you have between your grown and non-grown body. Almost a surgical join, a line of stitches.

As I understand it, you have a dick that you bought that you wear. It is your dick, despite spending time away from you. But then there is also this dick that is growing on your body, and I imagine that it is growing to meet the other and that there is a joining, and perhaps one, might take over the other? Not that there is a dick hierarchy. Wouldn't it be nice if we had words that honoured that process, or do you think I am creating hassle for no good reason?

Michael: No, not at all. We can only talk about where we currently are and for me the word 'dick', or 'cock' is very erotically charged. For me, I'm trying to imagine trying not to use those words for it.

I think one of my things about the word 'dick' used in a trans context is that many trans femmes will always have and use their birth genitals to fuck with and be fucked; so if we all employ the same word 'dick', it makes them feel/be perceived as incongruent. Likewise, if they have to simply call it a 'clit', then that feels quite fragile in terms of what we are asking the world to do to perceive or understand our bodies. If we have trans words (even 'transgina' is a start), then we build strong frameworks. We avoid 'chick with a dick'; we become segmented bodies.

Michael: I think there are two different things here. One is my personal arousal. It's very arousing for me to think of my body having a dick. That matters to me a lot, but then there is the stuff we put out in the world, how we describe ourselves.

It feels a little like we are stuck on pause, tackling and dismantling patriarchy with patriarchy. We do need to think longer term about community building – and not from the place of allies sheltering us from the storm, which is happening and currently very necessary – but community building which uses our own frames of reference, beyond the personal: the collective safe space. I think I describe my body beyond me, and I describe it to be recognised properly by external structures, healthcare, social structures and sexual structures. I feel like we are at the time of needing to move beyond the 'personal journey', however important or righteous it is, to community building. I think as elders we have a responsibility to at least get that ball rolling, a sliver of newly renamed space. This is about comfort, not rebelling.

Michael: But I still think that two things are going on here. One is the renaming to the world and then there is the personal 'How do I construct my body in terms of the erotic body?' I know they are not separate – we don't live in an isolated world – but I think they are two different things.

I think that your separation of them is true but also untrue, because it still relies on renaming the one fixed point: the body. We rename to have sex. We convince them that we are trans enough, not trans enough, that we have a cock that can fuck, a vagina that can be fucked, we're like them enough, we have tits that can be caressed or have a cock between them. Whatever it is, we rename our singular into their world. I agree with you that there is a congruence we build when we are alone but I'm not sure it's that easy to separate them out, else the link between perhaps the political body and the sexual body becomes quite fragile.

Michael: Yes, they are related, of course.

That's why I talk so much about wanking – to place the sexual and pleasurable trans body front and central into both a sexual and political space. My orifice is both feminist and political. My wanking is both depersonalised and politicised.

Michael: When you wank, is it at all gendered? Are fantasies or your perception of your body gendered or is it just physical sensation?

I'm trying to get to that point of just feeling and responding to my body. I suppose that's one of the trans delights for me is that my body is both old but reconfigured so works differently, pleasures differently. I stopped fancying cis men, which was a shock to me – I always pre-sumed I would; and trans bodies, for me, are uniquely individual and require touch, not fantasy. I no longer have thrusting cock fantasies. It stopped working for me on any level. It became too much like work, which doesn't work for wanking. So now I explore the space as both an erotic space but also a space with an unwritten narrative, and therefore touch and sensation really matter much more than fantasy. I feel much more embodied.

Michael: Most good orgasms are about being utterly in the body. The physiological, for me, is everything, but there is still the gendered component. Cock matters but I have no respect for patriarchy, just my masculine essence.

* * *

Talking with Michael about dicks and orgasms over breakfast feels perfect – my idea of a great date. Their brain, their consciousness and their sense of self, I love. I find it truly glorious that we met through a book, my book admittedly, but still a book. Chance or fate, I love how that shit happens. Michael talks about their masculine soul. They operate very much on that level of consciousness, in a space that entails going beyond the realms of comfort and uncomfortable to a space that is pragmatically ethereal. It's little wonder to me that everything between us feels easy, apart from kissing. We haven't kissed. We've talked about kissing but we haven't kissed. I don't think we will now but I love that they are in my life and I love being a part of theirs, so in a *quid pro quo* it feels like a very worthy exchange.

I like that this morning it felt like they interviewed me. It was fun. They always push me to extend my line of thinking beyond my comfort place to a place where it tests the idea. They're good at that. They have all the qualities that you would want to find in a friend or a lover. They're definite, upfront, caring and resolutely honest about my good points and my crap. There is no holding back. I love the companionship we are developing. It matters, especially for older people and even more for older trans folk. We need community. I'm very aware when I'm in Spain, in the mountains, that I far too often feel like one of one.

They've been talking about setting up more self-pleasure groups, perhaps one for the over-fifties. I'd still struggle to be in that shared space of singular self-pleasuring. I'm not sure why. I think I still have huge hang-ups about getting something right and not looking silly, which is silly considering the number of people that know everything about my life, my past and my genitals through my writing. On many levels I'm completely open and travel with confidence but I still really suffer from the idea that I'll get something wrong and parts of the sky might fall in. I suppose I feel safest in my writing. It feels like home and like a form of cathartic meandering towards a sanctuary.

Michael seems shy and perhaps more comfortable in small groups of people but they push their body and their sense of their body to places where they can discover new sensations and are comfortable exploring that with others. But it's very much on their own terms – they have really good boundaries. Maybe that's it – maybe I still don't trust that I have good boundaries. Maybe that's why I imagine that by getting it wrong I might spill out into the world and look silly. It's such a strange and uncomfortable paradox to live with. As a sex worker I sucked cock in phone boxes (it was the 80s and 90s, and phone boxes were still vital). I sucked cock and I knew that sometimes people could see. I didn't flinch. As a sex worker I engaged in group sex, group shows, I performed scenes and acted out others' fantasies.

I didn't flinch. Yet the thought of being vulnerable in a room of like-minded people terrifies me. But that's it, isn't it? I interpret the more dangerous one as being safe, and the safer space as being vulnerable.

That fucks my mind up still, I have to admit.

Earlier this year Michael came to visit me in Spain. It was spring and warm. They taught me yoga every day for a week in my courtyard and I cooked them food in return. I felt safe trying to balance and move more organically in front of them, and by the end of the week I replayed the week's teaching back to them in one session. I felt safe. It mattered to me.

Throughout my life I've so often felt body-vulnerable and constantly tried to find truth in the feelings associated with my body. Experimenting with BDSM throughout my twenties and thirties enabled me to realise that I did have limits. As a sub that was incredibly important, but letting go and being vulnerable has always felt like a step too far. It doesn't have to be sexual vulnerability but the fragility I or my mind associates with getting something wrong, not being able to follow clear instructions, feeling like I need to do everything perfectly.

I was once on holiday in Morocco with a lover and they became exasperated with me and said, 'Just let go, for fuck sake. Let go and stop caring what other people think of you.' We were walking out of the hotel, along the beach to the start of what I remember as mountains. He said to me, 'Just shout loudly here. Say anything you want –no one can hear you – just go.' To make matters worse, he demonstrated how to let go and shout with lungs full of air. He took an overly showy breath in and then boomed out a series of words as loud as he possibly could. And then he laughed and said, 'See how easy it is.'

I felt silly, diminished by his ability to let go. I couldn't do it and to this day here in the mountains around my home I still practise, and I still feel like I get it wrong. My voice never hits loud. I muffle myself even though there is no one for miles around to hear me. I'm forever trying to please or not displease an invisible being that sits on my shoulder.

Perhaps all those times that knowingly or inadvertently I exposed myself and my body to risk and harm did matter. Maybe it is their voices, their interactions, still with me and imprinted on my body. Maybe collectively they are the voices that I contend with. The ones that tell me I'm silly, undeserving and clumsy. I can countenance that. I can.

I was sexually assaulted by a man when I was fourteen years old. I was waiting at a bus stop to go home after a local drama lesson at a drama and dance club. It was a Saturday afternoon. The lesson was always Saturday morning. I was too shy for both drama or dance, but everyone thought it would be good for me and bring me out of my shell. My shell though was the suffocating misalignment of my gender. But how were they to know? I couldn't tell them – we didn't have the words then. My shell was my protection.

In the lessons – first drama, then dance – I stood at the back of the room, hoping and praying that I wouldn't get picked to perform. I could just about cope with acting as an inanimate object like a tree (in a school play I was once cast as a loaf of bread), or trying to follow the rudimentary steps of a dance routine at the back, but if called to the front, I froze.

Just froze.

At the bus stop I must have looked like the nervous teenager I was. He told me that the buses weren't working, that the drivers were on strike, but that he would help me out by giving me a lift home if I needed it.

'Do you live close?' he said.

He was older. He looked like a grandfather. We never had grandfathers in our family – they were both dead. Grandparents are painted by the world as being safe. I thought his car would be a safe space. I got into the pale green Cortina with beige seats.

I got in.

He abused me.

He told me, as he held me down, that I was a quick learner.

He dropped me off at a petrol station far from my home and I stood very still.

For a long time I stood very still and then I remained quiet even in the deserts of Morocco with a partner I trusted. I remained very quiet.

I never want to write about that again, ever, but words happen. These words just happened.

Michael has said to me, from the beginning of our friendship, that I could come along to one of the self-pleasure groups. I've never had the courage to say that although I've sucked cock in a phone box, on a street in Euston, for money, in front of strangers and felt nothing, the thought of being vulnerable in a safe space with like-minded people terrifies me.

I've said it now. I feel vulnerable and very happy that this chapter is over.

AMROU/ GLAMROU

I used to live in this part of London many years ago – the place where King's College Hospital meets the Maudsley Hospital. It's an inauspicious place, a junction really, which ironically, considering my life's current path, holds many memories for me. I used to come here weekly to attend a drug clinic, and each week, I'd say, 'I'm trying. I'm doing better.' I used to live at the top of Denmark Hill in a flat that was part of my rehab programme. Back then, twenty or thirty years ago, there actually was a drug rehab support network: programmes that were funded enough to support you over many years. It took me around ten years to get away from drugs and my drug-shaped life.

I'd leave the clinic each week with a smile and a script for methadone, walk a hundred yards towards Camberwell, sell it and then walk to a house a hundred yards in the opposite direction and buy heroin and crack cocaine. Many times I spent hours on the street, late at night or early in the morning, trying to randomly buy drugs; and just occasionally when times were hard I would try to sell sex near the station, the one I'm walking from this morning on my way to interview Amrou Al-Kadhi, the Iraqi-British nonbinary drag performer and writer.

Earlier this year they interviewed me about *Queer Sex*, and during the interview I found their ideas and concepts around gender and performance so interesting that I decided that if I did another book I would ask to interview them. The cusp of drag and trans identities and the resulting gendered expectations are fascinating in relation to the ways that it is ever so subtly shifting the parameters of gender, which in turn is leading to gender itself being ever so slightly toppled from its very fragile perch. It's not drag alone doing this but the whole plethora of gender identities that are converging over a wide plain and are fluid, nonbinary and queer.

They are challenging and reshaping the landscape in a way that binary trans identities often inadvertently merely add more to the existing binary frameworks. Both matter – the binary and the nonbinary – whatever works and gives ease to the individual matters. This isn't a 'binary trans blame game'. All trans folk challenge; but the more fluid the gendered identity, the more questions it asks, which in turn can create new space.

Walking to Amrou's, my mind is doing back flips trying to locate me as the person that walked these streets twenty or thirty years ago and me now, the writer, walking to interview one of the most successful performers and writers in our queer universe. They recently signed a six-figure deal for their memoir *Unicorn*. The deal was struck after a five-way auction. A queer book and a five-way auction... Queer hits the big time!

I wish I could pinpoint when and what exactly changed or allowed me to change. I can't pinpoint a single moment or a single thing that turned me around but I can pinpoint events, sometimes small and domestic and sometimes horrible and painful, that must have added up to me changing my life. There is nothing from my life then that I recognise in my life now.

I remember often feeling like I was losing my mind and being told that I *had* lost my mind. People assume that 'addicts' have no control whatsoever.

I was once forced to take a job, after a long stint in a rehab, to prove that I was clean and could stay clean enough to rejoin polite or impolite society. I had been stuck in a revolving door, in and out of rehabs, for many years and was testing the patience of the saintly people around me who really did want me to get clean and have a life. So many people suffer around one addict. So frustrating.

I looked at the list of jobs and for some reason (I was still secretly using drugs) decided that the lorry driver job seemed (bizarrely) sensible. I'm not a great driver, full stop, let alone a small lorry, but my mind just saw the time I'd spend alone in which I could sell, buy and score. It was one of the shortest periods of employment I've ever had. It consisted of me going in on a Monday to a paint factory in East London, lying and saying I understood about car engines (I couldn't even open the bonnet and after two weeks the engine seized due to my inability to top up the oil or water), and saying that early mornings weren't a problem for me (they weren't as I first used drugs at five in the morning to stop myself getting ill).

They gave me the job.

The paint factory was right next to a place where they killed chickens. I suppose it was a small poultry abattoir? There was always a terrible noise, and the smell of death wafted across in the early morning on the damp East London air. One morning a chicken ran into the yard, squawking, squealing and making fearful noises. It had momentarily escaped death.

A man who worked in the yard shifting great vats of industrial paint around saw it and looked at me.

'Do you like chicken?' he asked.

'Yes', I replied, thinking I like all animals (I think I prefer them to people).

In front of me, he grabbed it and snapped its neck and then tried to hand it to me. I moved away backwards, feeling nauseous, disgusted that my words, my causal, flippant words, had led to this. He threw the bird onto the grease- and paint-covered floor. The chicken lay there, convulsing with nerve energy coursing through its dead body. It seemed to be dad dancing and then it stopped and lay still. Against the paint it reminded me of that mixed media piece by Robert Rauschenberg.

'It's dead', he said. 'Pick it up, take it home and cook it.'

I walked out of the yard and back to the daily grind of addiction. I'd lasted two weeks and a day as a lorry driver. I'm amazed it was that long. I'm sure in my mind I used the chicken as an excuse for using drugs again but even here I cannot allow that lie to become truth. I used continually and walked out because any stress made me need to use drugs. The chicken joined the long list of things that, at that point in my life, I simply couldn't cope with, but it taught me a lesson.

The death of a single chicken destined for death that morning, anyhow, anyway, taught me that words matter, that each and every word of mine that left my mouth mattered and that once words exist in the world they cannot be taken back. Yes, I could express regret but, fuck, the chicken died then and there.

I know that the chicken would have died anyway, but my careless words caused its death when it had a slight chance of life, if only for a few extra minutes. I'm not powerful, but words are powerful.

It had only taken a 'yes' from me and the bird was dead. One word, one split second. Had I said, 'No, I love all living animals, please, let's set it free', then it would have turned out differently... or maybe not, but my one careless word enacted an easy death.

Back then people would say that I was 'a waste of space' or that I was 'beyond help'. People would talk about my mental instability. Only when I uttered the single word 'trans' in a therapy meeting about my addiction did some of my life make sense. The one word that needed to come out, came out.

I took that word and climbed back up and into a world that would not recognise me now as the person they wrote off back then. I'd been written off and verbally attacked without care.

Mentally unstable, mad, failed and forever broken.

Earlier this year Amrou was verbally abused on a crowded bus. People looked on but said nothing. They were called an 'abomination'. No one did a thing. A single word, which means 'an object of intense disapproval, shame, immorality or disgust'.

A single word.

* * *

I really want to talk to you about cocks. I don't know why, but I do. I think maybe when you interviewed me I got the sense that because you occupy two different performance spaces – your drag persona, Glamrou, and you as yourself – a cock might be, or might become, different things?

Amrou: It is. My cock... I have a very odd relationship with my own. Sometimes I'm very detached from it, very dysphoric. I see myself as a person, and the cock is just like, there, hanging on. It's taken me a long time, and actually I still don't think I am quite there, to fully see my cock as part of myself. So I used to find it strange when people were pleasuring my cock, like, 'Let me go down on you.' I couldn't even register it as pleasure because it didn't feel like it was part of me or something I could embody.

What did it feel like then? Was it pleasurable?

Amrou: Now it's pleasurable. Back then it was like, 'I'm just feeling saliva on this thing. I'm feeling it tingle but I don't even register it as pleasure in the moment.' I think it was gender dysphoria and maybe early ongoing 'this penis is a reminder of me failing as a man', because the way I was having sex in the gay male scenes, you're more attractive the more of a man you are, and I'm very femme and a person of colour.

But what happens is, when you are naked your identity dissolves a little bit to the person having sex with you. All of a sudden they are treating my cock.

I had to reclaim my cock and balls in order to feel embodied. I didn't expect that though. I assumed the word 'vagina' would work for me.

Amrou: White picket fence, woman.

Yes, but the opposite happened. Once I reclaimed it, it felt that it was society that should do some work, not just me to fit into them. I couldn't and didn't fit.

When you're naked, does identity fall away or does the naked cock, with all of its attributed meanings and performance expectations, take over?

Amrou: That's a really interesting question. I'm someone who finds I'm so attached to clothes, make-up, expression and language, I don't see them as things I'm adding on. I see them as part of me, as part of my DNA in expressing myself, and suddenly when I'm naked I lose all of my defences. I find, being really honest here, because I used to feel so dysphoric from my penis I would premature ejaculate, very, very quickly because I wasn't in control of it. It didn't feel like it was fused to my body.

I think there are, or were, many things going on there, because I was bought up in the Middle East where it is a really gendered society. Technically it is. Men pray in one room, women in another. Even the language is really gendered: verbs change, even sounds. The way that your mind operates is that there are things for men and things for women. I felt so detached from the men around me and so attached to my mother and the women in my life, that I think that maybe it took me a really long time to reclaim my penis as being part of who I can be now.

A kind of cultural detachment?

Amrou: Yes, a real cultural detachment. It's also to do with gay shame and sex. There is something I find quite basic about a penis. It's quite binary – it's on or it's off. You're there or you're not. That's not how my mind is or my identity is, but all of a sudden I'm naked and the only thing that someone can read is 'on or off' and it feels so distant from who I am, and I feel so detached from it.

It operates, or responds, on its own.

Amrou: Yes, on its own.

The binaries are set. When 'on', the cock inhabits this massively gendered, macho, machismo patriarchy.

Amrou: All of which ruined my teenage life. In drag I know what I want to get from space. But all of a sudden a cock is on or off. So detached. I don't attach sexual pleasure to my penis that much. Yes, I can come, but sexual pleasure for me comes from desire and I never fantasise about someone's penis.

So you don't fantasise about other cocks?

Amrou: It's complicated because I am attracted to men, including trans men, so it isn't just about a cock.

Is it masculinity?

Amrou: I'm not just attracted to masculine people. Initially gayness was a segue into queerness, which was a segue into nonbinary identity, but when I'm in gay male spaces I find it so patriarchal and so at odds with everything else. But those are the only situations where, for the most part, I am having sex. The way that people desire me is really bizarre.

I'd like to come back to that but I just wanted to ask you about your use of the word 'defences'. It feels – your persona and your drag – more like a celebration than a defence, but did it become celebration and before that what were you defending against?

Amrou: Initially when I started doing drag, about eight years ago, really inhabiting and manipulating the way I looked and having fun expressing myself, initially, for me, drag was pure escapism but not productive. It felt almost like the way addicts escape.

I'd arrived at university suffering from gay shame because of the way I was brought up and the rejection I felt. I didn't know how to have sex. Two seconds in, I'd come. I hadn't resolved any of it. I'd always been quite confident in myself though, which feels complicated but it's true. I decided to try drag and I started a drag night. All of a sudden I became like a drag prophet. I felt powerful, I felt like I could be rude and sexy but not sexual. I was performing being sexy. I've never felt sexy. I felt like flailing limbs, not a man, and that's what I thought sexy was back then: a man. But when the drag came off, it was almost like it was almost a lie, so it felt quite schizophrenic: in drag, confident about sex and my identity; out of drag, terrified about sex, terrified about intimacy. It was almost as if (I talk about it like failed hypnosis) I could just tell myself something. I was using drag as a way to pause reality.

Did you have sex in drag?

Amrou: One time with a cis guy in a nightclub but not penetrative sex. But that was more recent, and drag doesn't feel separate now. Back then, drag felt like a fake orgasm, a way to not deal with anything.

I wonder, because you said that you felt sexy but not sexual, often it feels like quite a linear join between sexy and sexual, as you create space around you based on feeling sexy, a confidence. I sometimes feel that I create a different kind of space around me when I feel sexy or attractive. Cis men, especially, respond. That feels quite basic.

Amrou: They are basic.

I wonder what happened to that sense of sexy self when you came out of drag?

Amrou: At first I felt uglier out of drag. Back in the day, drag felt like a second closet.

What was drag the closet for? What were you coming out into?

Amrou: Queer and gender nonconforming. But my parents couldn't find out about my drag, so I hid it literally in the closet. But also gay men, on the whole, are so femme-phobic. So I was like, 'Drag is something I'll do in private', which is bizarre as drag is such a public 'look at me' thing, and then I'd make sure that my nail polish wasn't on and my wigs were away. I don't do that now but back then I did. I'm more public now, so I know that they will know.

The more success I had as a sexual drag queen or like someone who was performing sexiness, the more gay men were like, 'We live for you but we don't find you sexual.'

I sometimes think that about our allies in the sense that they stake out our rights alongside of us but how many of them truly see us as sexual? Sometimes, when allies or potential allies say, 'What can I do to support you?', I say, 'Fuck me.' They laugh nervously but remain silent. They remain our allies over the other side of the glass, which can only mean they don't see us as real on a sexual level. It feels reductive and faintly patronising. I don't need them to have my back from that distance – too much can slip between. We come together over a leaflet or a campaign.

Amrou: Can you desire me?

Yes. I honestly wonder if that is a robust seam.

Amrou: My dating life is tough because of this. There are some guys, cis white guys, who have met me in drag, a person of colour in drag. They desire me. I think there is some eroticisation going on in terms of my colour.

I think they think, 'I can own this femme person of colour.'

Then their masculinity will go from strength to strength. They think they can fuck me. They doubt my agency. Then we meet up and they find out that I am funny, clever and successful – all the things they see as masculine. Then they use my success as a way to shut me up, like I might talk about a film I'd like to make, and they say, 'Why are you talking about making a film when I hate my job?' As a femme person of colour, my inhabiting any structures of masculinity, which they perceive as their birthright, quite literally turns them off.

One guy just stopped messaging me. He couldn't cope with the idea that I might be a top in life by their terms of reference. He was so attractive, it was hard not to be attracted to him when you have been made to feel completely unattractive your whole life by their terms of reference again. We'd gone on one date and I talked, like we are talking now, and I could see the cogs going in his head at a hundred miles an hour as he thought, 'I can't own you, I don't know how to desire you, you're feminine but I'm not sure you will submit.'

I felt punished by them. It often feels like a power move on their part. I know that as gay men we are oppressed, but many of them have whiteness; white men are so entrenched with structures of privilege. I remember one man saying, 'I'm sorry, the drag is freaking me out. I'm attracted to men.'

Such a weird statement – where does men go in their eyes? Do you desire the potential performance of a cock and that overrides everything else real in the room? Does a cock have that much power? Are we really that basic? I've changed my dating profile to reflect my genital truth. People always ask, 'Have you had surgery?' and I reply, 'Yes, they reconfigured my cock and balls.' That is my truth. They say, 'I'm not interested.' But if I'd said, 'Yes I have a vagina', they'd want to fuck. Same space, different words, my truth. There is something inherently magical about being trans. I'm tired of hiding that in their reductivity and performance needs. It's a little like drag: drag destabilises masculinity.

Amrou: Totally. I always say that drag is like going, 'Hi the jig is up.' In terms of the Middle East, where I and my family were raised, life is often about keeping up appearances, often to quite shocking levels. People will get angry at me if they know that someone in the community has seen me in pink socks. And it's not about the pink socks. It's a drag show.

Middle-Eastern families have a real sense of collective responsibility. Especially because we came from Iraq and were in London during the war in Iraq, we needed to stay together, like cultural territorialism. There was the silent agreement that we all need to do the same thing; everyone does what everyone else is doing; all men do the same things. Masculinity is really tough for cis men as they have to play the game. For me it was simply like, 'Game over. I'm nowhere near it.'

My gayness and drag were shame that didn't fit with their notion of men living like kings.

There are these performances that happen. Normativity creates these swirling performances, such as masculinity, femininity, respectability, successfulness. People simply oscillate between those mini performances and never stand still. It's exhausting. A gradual collecting of signifiers and words to prove anchoring.

Trans is my destination and I'm not sure it has many performances, as trans has been historically labelled as second-rate and a space to constantly move away from. Are the performances between here and there, the cultural performances around sexuality, in any way similar or vastly different. What is the difference in the role of a cock?

Amrou: I'll come back to cocks there, and answer the first question. I think I present a different performance as I'm Middle Eastern, femme and successful. That excludes me because it blows apart the accepted performances and the notions of success.

How is it that this femme person is taking up way more space than they should and I am? That is the same there and on the gay scene. The idea that a femme person, a femme person of colour, should take up any space is still relatively new. I literally feel that, like somehow my being calls bullshit on their structures.

I sometime feel that my being present on the gay scene as a femme person of colour who plays with drag can literally castrate the men who find me attractive, because of their attachment to masculinity. I can see them thinking, 'Am I not into men anymore?' People hate their bullshit being called.

I think that can be the same on the trans scene, as so few people's performances are ever deemed good enough to be allowed into a normative space. Many of the rest of us are almost punished for trying too hard or not hard enough, even from inside the community. I often get trans people, especially femme trans women of a certain age, calling me out because they say I destabilise their access into normativity. Certainly my non-use and rejection of the words 'woman' and 'vagina' often appear to be wrongly read as me trying to rock the boat in which we are all supposed to sit, which is bullshit as I am simply labelling my own boat. People like numbers, that's power, a numbers game. Trans has been packaged as a position of oscillation, with us trying to fit their model and being bounced away to try again, back and forth.

Amrou: That's not a great place to inhabit.

No, unless you can re-label trans as the destination, and then you can quieten down the noise of oscillation to a point where you can breathe and see where it is you are standing. Trans becomes the resting and residing space. It's a lack of performance that could inform us. We only rename to enter their space and the space of gender. I feel slightly sorry for cis men who are trapped under years and years of clinging on to the centre, trying desperately to be a man. The world would be far happier trans.

Amrou: As they fail, they punish others. Fuck masculinity.

If they punish enough of us, it defines their distance or closeness to 'successful' gender norms. Their masculinity is defined by being 'nothing like them'. It reminds me slightly of nonbinary status.

Amrou: And then it throws them all for six when they end up desiring you.

Absolutely. They get anchored to the wrong side - in their eyes.

Amrou: I find it incredibly basic. I'm like, 'Why don't you just trust the desire that's happened, because that's really honest: You want to fuck me and I want to fuck you.' Men have an idea of what and who they can desire, but that gets in their way. That's why I love drag; because it's performing to unperform. Initially I think drag was bad for me as it was a fake performance. I was unhappy and unconfident. Now drag to me is like dishonest honesty. It's like, here are my wears and tears, this is what I feel I look like sometimes. It's very vulnerable. My drag can become quite upsetting. I inhabit a side of myself that feels honest. Drag allowed me to do it. Now when I take off my drag I don't feel too much distance from what has happened. Back in the day, Glamrou used to be a white woman. I didn't realise it at the time, but she just wore what white women wear in the media and I was so detached from my heritage.

I was going to ask you if Glamrou has changed as you have?

Amrou: Yes. Glamrou used to be a white, secular woman who was out to kill Amrou. I was in the West thinking 'fuck religion' as I felt Islam had really hurt me. But then it changed. So much about Islam runs deep within me and so much of it I love. Islam has a lot of queerness within it. But back at the start I felt so detached, so that version of Glamrou represented that detachment. Then really slowly, through so much self-actualisation, reading and other work, Glamrou started to pull out stuff about Amrou that I'd forgotten about; for example, how much I love the Middle East. Glamrou is a Middle-Eastern woman; she's like my mum. Through Glamrou I discovered my nonbinary identity. Before, I thought: boy, Amrou; girl, Glamrou. I think I was just adhering to cis normative standards, cis images of femininity. Now they have really merged for me.

Glamrou seems like much more of a 'being', like a composite idea of something other than gender. Your 'sea' film makes perfect sense to me. Glamrou seems otherworldly. Trans doesn't have a celebrated, desirable performance as we have been told that trans is an identity to grow away from. I sometimes think that Glamrou is a perfect trans performance, unbroken and empowered.

Amrou: Trans could rule the world. I love the idea of drag

changing the space around it. I see drag as an aesthetic propo-
sition of what the world could be.

*I really relate to Glamrou's drag. I never have related to other drag –
perhaps because I did gay really badly. People would tell me that: 'You
do gay really badly.' I adore some of the new drag which genuinely
pushes and pulls at frontiers. It feels like we can take the edges of
gender and have fun with them and define them.*

Amrou: When I'm in drag and taking up space and altering space,
it feels like I can be a species that others haven't encountered.
What I find odd about the cock question is that my cock is still
there, but (and I don't know who is doing the castrating) I feel
and see the audience pull away slightly. I have gay men saying
thank you for what I said on stage, but they pull away sexually. I
feel like saying, 'I can whip my cock out and you can suck it, it's
fine, it's still here.' I enjoy the otherworldly feeling on stage, but
if I come out into the bar still in drag then people feel confused.

*Older drag was very binary and reductive femininity. Lots still is.
Glamrou isn't. It's very un-'Drag Race'. Glamrou breaks that down.
Does a nonbinary cock have an understood performance yet, does
it have erotic currency? I don't have the words yet to describe my
genitals and it feels like they lack easy-breezy trading value.*

Amrou: It's funny you should say that. Someone said to me the
other day that maybe I should go on a different dating app. They
said, 'What do you call a gay man who fancies a nonbinary male
body, because they're not gay anymore are they?'

The structures of language on Tinder, etc. exclude us and our fluidity and changes.

People fancy static as a space they inherently add to. Trans isn't pinned down yet, even the trans that does normativity beautifully. I think people want to stay still – it makes sense in a short life. People don't want to let go of that.

Amrou: I don't understand why people wouldn't want to let go of that. Those spaces don't work for anybody. The system feels so safe for people though.

Our naked bodies seem to still get co-opted into that stuff. We have to get hold of the space that opens up around our naked bodies. I wonder how your naked body, your cock, fits into this space. Do erections work for you now? You said earlier that they present a dilemma.

Amrou: Yes, it works for me a lot better now because I have conceptualised my identity and my body in a certain way. What I maybe struggle with is not how I perceive my own cock but how others perceive it. When I go to sex parties in New York and I'm just naked – the reason I have very specific tattoos which continue that drag on my skin is to say that this isn't a neutral body, but naked I am an Arab man with a big cock – people read me as an Arab dom top, whatever my performance.

Cocks aren't one thing, they are a range of performances. They are power and non-power depending on shape, size, etc.

Amrou: I think people think, 'There is Arab with big dick so therefore cisgender dom top.' I can be a dom top but on my own terms, not cisgender terms. I like being a top. When I'm naked and people don't know anything about Glamrou, then my body is read as sexual.

Just the body being the controlling factor?

Amrou: I can have great sex, I have to admit. The whole top and bottom question is strange. Because I failed at society's idea of masculinity, I was supposed to be a bottom. It's so binary.

Yes, being a bottom is often presented as a failed model of top, a second-rate space. It's so silly.

Amrou: An exploration of prostates works for everyone.

I think that trans bodies occupied and embodied fully are such sites of power. Can Glamrou ever work as a naked body?

Amrou: I would hope so. I feel like my experiences dating and the rejection of my femininity in dating makes it hard. I feel like I would have to find someone who is up for knowing all parts of me. Gay male anonymous sexual spaces are where I have most of my sex and it feels quite separate from Glamrou. Those spaces can leave me feeling like I have had to pretend to do masculinity. Once Glamrou is present on my Tinder, the matches plummet. If it is just Arab man, then I get much more interest. I hope Glamrou can become part of a desirable destination.

We still exist in such a fragile space.

Amrou: I want to be like a sea creature that embodies all sexes in one nonbinary form.

* * *

'Cock' is a fairly short, four-letter word but one that I'm beginning to realise has many meanings in and around our trans lives. Words matter. Cock isn't just one thing: his cock, their cock, her cock, proprioceptive cock, she kept her cock, he is getting his cock, a cock on the shelf, a cock in a harness, a cock being used to create a neo-vagina.

There are many states, meanings, constructions and different power states:

The 'cock' depicted in porn as the ploughing object that thrusts through scene after scene, relentlessly fucking, be that a trans cock or a cis cock, when in truth we know that many porn scenes are held up for hours on end with stagefright cocks trying to achieve erections.

The cock tucked high and tight between the cheeks of a drag queen, hidden masculinity apparently, squashed between arse cheeks. The cock seen as a male thing to be hidden, tapped up, in order for femininity to work, to be alone on display. Its power, its desirability, it potential to fuck changed?

Is the cock that lines my orifice the same as the one before that stood out and defined me as male? I still rely on the erectile tissue for pleasure, so how different is it? It's unrecognisable as a cock but still it is cock tissue, cock skin, cock blood supply, and cock veins, arteries and capillaries. It is the ultimate in feminine encasement for the totemic masculine symbol.

A cock-made-cunt made beautifully trans, a cock-made-cunt open to description right across the spectrum; to some simply a 'vagina', to some a 'transgina', to me, yet to be named.

My genitals remind me of drag, genitals in drag, I like the fluidity away from a fixed binary point. It's my truth that my cock is still there, albeit massively altered and reconfigured, but essentially it still lies there, stitched in position, just the balls completely removed. It's wonderfully trans, transgressive; but most importantly to me, it's not an act of rebellion or activism, it's both comfort and mellow. My genitals, my cock and balls, in this current configuration, afford me joy, ease and a sense of self that I have never experienced before.

A mellow cock-fashioned femme.

It can be interpreted in a myriad of ways. Some see it simply as a vagina like any other vagina, and why not? Structurally they're very much the same. The genital construction of male and female sex organs under the skin are incredibly similar; and as no two vaginas are the same, it's a good bet that a trans vagina can be like any other. But, for me, my empowerment and autonomy come from owning its history lock, stock and cock.

I adore Amrou's drag incarnation Glamrou. There is no using the feminine to hide the masculine, just the detoxification and alteration of the masculine by the adoption and playful inquisition into feminine and cultural stereotypes and narratives. Hairy legs and a hairy chest placed alongside sequins, with no attempt to allow one to dominate another. This isn't irony or toxicity but an incarnation of fluidity and honourable homage. It's not the 'fishiness' so often used in 'Drag Race' to define and ironically denigrate the feminine – so much toxic masculinity used to ramp up a man's idea of their ability to occupy the space of woman.

Amrou's drag spells out its objection to the objectification of women through costume. A big cock, often talked about, is tucked up between their legs but is still there, just behind fabric. No sense of pyramidal falsified perfection aspired towards. This is political drag that demands much else other than belief in the false-feminine.

The man on the bus called Amrou and Glamrou an 'abomination'.

To him I say, 'Shut the fuck up!'

It's the trans and nonbinary communities taking gender and detoxifying it for 'future societies' to exist within more freely and more joyfully. His children and grandchildren will all benefit from this. We're doing the work that you lot have neglected to do for centuries and centuries, preferring to simply occupy the sliver of powerful space gender afforded you as cis men. White cis men. I know that to be true because before this part of my life I appeared to be a white cis man and that was enough to allow me to occupy the sliver of luxurious privilege that exists in that space. Privilege isn't actually a physical thing like a rock or a stone but privilege is so powerful that it enables and often encourages rocks, stones and burgers to be thrown.

How dare they shout insults at Amrou or throw burgers at Travis when it is they who are changing the world, detoxifying the world, for all of us.

To the man shouting insults or the man throwing a burger, I say, 'You are not the gifts.' Travis's words: 'You are not the gifts.'

It is the trans, fluid, nonbinary and queer folk, often led by queer and trans people of colour, who are the gifts and are doing this work now whilst the parts of society, the parts that exist in the privileged gender-slivers, hiss and spit at us for taking away their slivers of power.

Trans nonbinary and gender nonconforming people of colour are at the sharp edge of this fight and they need all our support. To do this we must recognise our privilege and not define our struggles as being the same. They cannot extinguish a better future if we all stand in authenticity together.

My cock is still there – unrecognisable maybe, but it gives me pleasure – and naming it aloud allows me to feel whole away from the stupidity and reductivity of the binary gender pillars, which are, if you look close enough, beginning to crumble ground up. Look closer and you'll see the trans community in all of its breadth bravely taking them down, brick by brick.

My own version of drag, there between my legs, isn't artifice or pretence. It is the perfect blend of cock and now, to the world, vagina. Every bit of trans surgery is an act of rebellion against the history and herstory of this gendered world. I exist as a trans person because I have taken gender by the balls and made it work for me, not me for it.

Twenty or thirty years ago, people saw me as a disordered being – incongruent on the street, a junkie, a queer, a person who had AIDS and who was mentally unstable – rather than simply seeing me as a work in progress just starting, a person at the start of a journey that requires immense bravery.

Trans folk are beautiful.

Amrou and Glamrou are perfectly colliding, aligning, twisting and turning like the sea creature of their fantasy. They are beautifully weaving a new story of gender that takes that privileged sliver and forces it wide apart. Watch them run in laughing, full of ease and joy, the people made safe by Amrou and Glamrou.

E-J SCOTT

I was trying to locate and interject, as a peaceful form of protest, trans history into the museum — almost as a form of activism, curating as a form of activism, but what I couldn't do with this exhibition was locate trans history from the past.

E-J Scott

E-J Scott established and curates the wonderful Museum of Transology. He is brilliantly astute, engagingly bright and acutely aware of his personal space and the public space around him that evolves by E-J being a 'him', by being a man, a genderqueer trans man, but a man nonetheless. He sees the Museum of Transology as a means to peacefully protest – that's the kind of wonderful he is.

I first saw him being interviewed by Grayson Perry as part of Grayson's series on masculinity. In it, E-J talked about being uncomfortable occupying 'man' when it still has such a plethora of privilege and toxicity. He was one of the most open and radical voices in the whole series. The next time I saw E-J was in person at the Trans and Nonbinary Conference at The University of Brighton a few years ago. I was giving the morning's keynote. I saw E-J and we hugged. It was a great conference, and that made complete sense to me considering that the person organising the event, E-J, should be so reflective about their own identity and be able to use that as a starting-point for wider enquiries and investigations about the world around us.

It's the kind of quality you seldom find in people: the ability to be reflective before speaking and then formulating opinions or standpoints. Great teachers aren't simply experts in their own fields but also have the ability to reflect at length on their teaching practice and methods. Being an expert isn't enough if you wish to share expertise or knowledge. E-J's work, be that through the Museum of Transology or the work they do at the Tate, is accessible, tactile and emotionally open because they know, as all great teachers and communicators do, that to reach people you first have to respect and then trust them. Almost universally in this queer universe of ours, if you talk of E-J, people have only positive things to say about his generosity of spirit but also the tenacity of his queerness.

E-J's is my last interview. It wasn't planned to be – it's just how it's turned out – but it feels right that it is. When I walk into his shared house, it feels right.

The noise of his dogs barking makes me miss my own who bark endlessly in an untrained (I did try) fashion whenever a soul comes near to my house. My dogs live in Spain most of the time, principally because there they can run free in the mountains but also because there are far fewer people to bark at. That's the net result of my training methods: move to the middle of nowhere. Ruby, the smaller of my dogs, has taken to barking at any movement or noise, including the weather if it's anything other than the normal, silent, sunny days. The rain or wind are all reasons for her to bark now. Ruby barks and Max, my larger dog, follows. I'm sure their chorus can be heard across the valley and up into the mountains. They are both rescues, so I make allowances for their tougher beginnings but I'm mortified by my inability to train them.

E-J's dogs' barking makes me think about Ruby and Max in kennels in Spain. Max is happy anywhere, but Ruby dislikes being anywhere but home or my mum's house in the U.K. I love collecting them and taking them home. It's genuinely a joyful time.

E-J's interview is the final interview for this book. After him, the interview process is over. Tomorrow morning I fly home to put the book together. I have about six or eight weeks to finish it and hand it in.

I've written three books over the past three years, two complete outlines and far too many articles, essays and talks to mention. I fucking love words and I adore being in the process of writing. It's like a relationship and I can already sense the day I will hand this book in and end the relationship. I'm a creature-of-habit writer. I work in the same way when planning a book, writing a book and editing the book. Every writing day follows the same rituals and timetable.

I start each day by reading and editing the writing from the day before, with a large milky cup of turmeric chai. After that I map out on A3 paper where I want or think I want to go that day. If I am transcribing an interview, I just get on with it. I edit as I transcribe – it's a process I could never hand over to anyone.

Two of the books I have written have been published or are going to be published, the third I have put on the back burner as I need to sit with it for a while longer and maybe do some re-writes. My head is full of ideas for books and essays that I want to write. Writing gives me peace and no peace. Writing is my constant companion now.

My energy is low and I'm feeling slightly stressed because for some reason (I don't know why) I have only allowed an hour to do the interview with E-J, from start to finish. That never happens. I always allow masses of time: a morning, an afternoon or even a day to carry out an interview. Having enough time before and after really matters and really informs the interview. But with E-J I have an hour, so I set the alarm on my phone. A car is picking me up in exactly one hour, and it's a street you can't easily park on. I need to focus. I have so many questions but I know from experience that the interview will lead the way rather than my set of questions.

E-J sits on a vast sofa covered in hand-knitted throws that I covet, and I sit opposite them in an incredibly comfortable armchair. I look at them and realise that I find them physically attractive. They have the most beautiful face: slightly cheeky but also wistful and poetic. I wish we had more time, but it's an hour, so I start.

* * *

I saw you a couple of years ago on television chatting to Grayson Perry, I think it was his series on masculinity, on what it means to be a man in today's society. I was struck by what you said as you introduced a different angle, one that felt politically queer but also quite vulnerable in amongst the other quite binary discussions around men.

E-J: I was questioning the role that I play in reinforcing gender normativity, because I do sit with the pronoun 'he' and I do present as male and my transness is about that, so I felt an increasing discomfort that binary transness is being located as binary. I don't see me identifying as he and presenting as a man as being hetero-cis normative; it's still trans masculinity and there is nothing fucking binary about me because I'm trans, so I have reshaped my body to be like this, I have gone through a hormone shift, a shift in my physicality because of my hormone treatment. This has brought me closer to being outwardly pre-senting in a way that I am comfortable with in an expression of my gender; but it is simplistic and problematic when people locate that and think that because I'm not identifying as non-binary I must be identifying as binary. I can't be binary – I cut my tits off.

So in what way does that make me present as a cis norma-tive man who's reinforcing masculine stereotypes? I disagree. I think actually it's extraordinarily radical to cut your body off, to make it fit how you want to present; and I think it's even being misread by my own trans community that I am becoming part of the problem because I am presenting as he.

I agree. I see everything I have done – surgery and hormones – as being trans-affirming and not-anything-else-affirming. I only encountered problems when I thought it might be binary-affirming. For me, that led me nowhere.

E-J: I still struggle with that. I'm going to be open and not hide. I can't hide the fact that I still would describe my experience as being dysphoric. I would describe my craving to be a man as very, very real and deeply unsettling for me, and nothing that surgery has been able to solve or hormones have been able to solve. It's been a very, very, slow painful road to me being able to say 'I am trans', and it's still hard for me. I can have all the politics in the world, I can be entirely proactive, I can be radical in my activism; and I consider myself to be radical because I am proactive, right, in a way that I am trying to create a seat in the world for other trans people to hopefully have it easier than I had when I grew up in a shitty little country town in Australia where the gay kids used to hang themselves from the same tree every year – that's what I grew up with. I am very motivated to create a different space for trans people by exposing a level of normativity and everydayness and a celebration of the difference of it, but certainly in a way that all things creative should be celebrated – not in a 'look this is different' way, but rather as 'everything is beautiful in the world and the more exciting and creative and expressive and explosively remarkable it is, then the more wonderful it is'. I think in society we have this idea that we have to quash difference and normalise it. I'm not trying to achieve that kind of space but am trying to open up the everydayness and say that it is like a blooming flower in spring: it's vibrant, it's colour, it adds to the texture of life, it's humanity.

I like to talk more at some point about that small Australian town and your beginnings.

When I first saw you with Grayson, I experienced you as brave and perhaps even 'blooming' – your term – in amongst people still seeking to define or redefine masculinity using only normative struc-tures. Listening to you talk now and knowing your work, I wonder how does the rising or ever-present dysphoria in seeking masculinity still remain?

E-J: It is nothing I have been able to solve. I don't aspire to hyper-masculinity. That's possibly what gets confused by labelling a trans person 'binary'. In actual fact, masculinity is wonderful in its flexibility, and growing what it means is what is progressive and exciting about it.

My identity is genderqueer, my identity is queer, my trans-ness is secondary to that. It's the transness I struggle with emotionally because I would like to not take medicine every day, I would like to have not had surgery, I would like to have a functioning sexual body in the way that I wish it was (just *carte blanche* 'here you go, you're born, grow up and have sex just as you are'). I would have liked that freedom.

And ease?

E-J: Yes, and ease. 'Ease' is a better word. I am one of the people that can never have surgery that works. I will never have a functioning erect penis for a number of medical reasons: I'm too skinny, currently the operation doesn't exist for me, I will never have sensation, etc. I will never get this body that I would like to play with. That's the seed of my anxiety.

You said something which feels quite radical: that masculinity can be a beautiful thing.

E-J: To think that trans men who identify as men fit into a box of hyper-normativity is to lack vision for the potentiality of transness. It is actually that we can be an aspirational new model of masculinity that is not toxic. This is our opportunity to shape ourselves into the form of masculinity in which we are proud to live. I live very openly. I'm very conscious to acknowledge that I did grow up as a girl. That was not my experience but that was my socialisation and I challenge anyone who says that does not inform my feminism, my understanding of masculinity, the toxicity and privilege of masculinity all of which I lived underneath when I was living in this tiny little sexist, homophobic town with hyper-masculine cowboys (literally, men from the outback who rode horses, drove trucks and raised cattle). That form of masculinity is incredibly problematic. My opportunity to shape my own masculinity through this process has allowed me to shape a set of morals, politics, ethics and behaviours that I try and adhere to as a man who challenges the patriarchy and challenges of heteronormativity. This is one of the things that transness has opened up to me. I also encourage my cis male friends to challenge these models and be feminists, and they do and it's simplistic to say that they don't. I like to think that my transness informs the kind of guy I am just as much as my little queer dyke background informs my feminism. These are all parts of my puzzle that make up my life experiences, and inform my politics and who I am and the way in which I aspire to live my life healthily and impact on radical positive change.

Your truth feels like this incredibly dignified, interwoven position. But the ongoing dysphoria you talk about from having a trans body, from not having a cock that might give closure, is tough to hear. How important is a cock to this, to your, whole story?

E-J: It's so difficult for me to understand because I wish I could wish it away. I wish my trans body could be everything to me in the way that I see the most wonderful trans people being able to come to terms with their body. It just hasn't ever proven to be emotionally possible for me.

An emotional disconnect?

E-J: Yes, it makes it very difficult to have satisfying sex. Believe me, I'm not scared about sex, about radical sex and trying everything, but I have an intense longing for a different body. That makes me feel unfulfilled in a way that I can almost absolutely not fucking explain. It's a bit heartbreaking for me because I have tried so hard in so many different ways for so long.

Just to put that in time context, can we have a potted E-J history starting in that small Australian outback town?

E-J: Knew I was trans from a very young age, always dressed in boys' clothes, wouldn't wear skirts, wouldn't wear dresses, screamed blue murder if my mum tried to make me. All of these classic stories which are a bit simplistic, but that's the truth of it. I was in boys' clothes as soon as I hit five or six in the late 70s, as soon as I was allowed to ride a skateboard or BMX. I only partook in boys' activities.

I didn't have any words to describe me, I didn't know any trans people, so I came out as queer and identified as queer to lovers and friends; but I always talked about 'androgyny' and the 'third gender', those kinds of terms.

Transitioned mid- to late-twenties, twenty odd years ago.

I left Australia and went to live in Tokyo where the boys are shorter, androgynous and small like me, a place where I could fit in.

I had to get my drugs on the black market. I'd go up this sky-scraper in Tokyo, all the way up in the lift to an apartment. This little slot would open up and they'd look at me through it and see it was me. I'd pass through money and then they'd close it and let me in. I'd have to take all my clothes off and put on a gown, lie down and wait for this Japanese doctor to come in fully suited as if for surgery (medical gloves and a gown). Then he'd inject me in my arse and I'd leave. This went on for a couple of years.

Such a cinematic image.

E-J: I had to run away from everything in my life in Australia because none of that would have been possible.

I have reframed my life now in the sense that I can see that actually I was born trans, not female or male but trans. I wonder what is my relationship to gender and if I need to have a relationship with gender. I often think, now, that the truth of gender actually resides in trans folk in that we make it work for us rather than being enslaved to it.

Do you think trans people can change the world?

E-J: I think they are. I went to Charleston yesterday, the home of the privileged queer artists. They have just done an extension and they have gender neutral signs on the doors. On the way home I was talking to my nonbinary friend in the car and they were saying that their brother just thinks we're mad and he will never get us. I said to them, 'But he can't deny that there are now gender neutral toilets. They exist, they are structures.' Little by little we are unpacking and unseating what gender is supposed to mean and I think that it is inevitable. I think that's where the transphobic backlash comes from: what is largely, traditionally, a radical left-wing feminist group which is now embracing Alt-right perpetuation of misinformation, an Alt-right tactic. For these left-wing women to be embracing far-right tactics speaks volumes about their disconnect, not ours. What is it that they are trying to protect so much that they turn their backs on the ethics of their approach? These are 'academics'. It is a sign that, at the very least, trans people are disrupting. And that disruption is the earthquake which lets off the fumes from shifting tectonic plates – fumes which stink until new life is born.

It's been so centred on genitals, cocks really, the lack of 'real' vagina is really raising the spectre of missing cock. It's incredibly reductive, so not only is their stance bankrupt in relation to their own ethical standpoint but it reduces all of us to cocks and cunts or cocks and non-real cunts. By all of us, I mean all of us – all of society is lessened by this debate.

I use the words 'reconfigured cock and balls' to reclaim and to have some authority and autonomy on and in my body and my process – social and surgical. Those words also allow me to access real pleasure as 'gendered parts' – 'vagina' always made me feel that I was failing. But our surgeries are based on looking like them, having perfect 'functional' cocks and vaginas. I wonder if we disconnected from that normativity and thought much more about pleasure and shape. I wish that we didn't feel so broken by not having normative genitals. Do you think we can reshape that genital debate and our own genital process(es)?

E-J: I'm working on reshaping that. I think I've made a slight shift in the last year or two, and it's been through a lot of care and attention from radical trans queers who I have in my life that are absolute role models and teach me more and more about it... People like Serge Nicholson. Talking to Serge about new ways of understanding what sex is just gives me a little bit of hope. I can celebrate intimacy being a hand on my back, on my naked skin, and think about the sensation that causes and allow myself to be titillated by that, and find new erogenous zones, finding different ways to reframe my genitals. I've always called my genitalia by masculine names, but by reframing how I use speech about my entire body so it all can become erogenous and not just located in my genitalia. I play with that to open up and reshape.

But at the end of the day I do think that a lot of us do have a great big blanket over us that has been the normativity. The overexposure to porn and all of the body beauty stuff that everyone in this fucking world goes through, it's a very heavy blanket to lift.

It's taken me years. I used to try and walk like a cowboy to please my dad and masculinity. Man and boy never worked for me, but the only dysphoria, proper dysphoria, I ever had and felt deep down was after surgery when people would say, 'That looks so real' or 'You'd never know in a changing room'. Trying to occupy a space that looked real rather than one that felt real freaked me the fuck out. But it's been a journey of years, decades. Ironically, the female bits that looked real had very little feeling; the expanse of erectile tissue they left behind that they were going to remove was the bit with feeling and sensation. That felt like such a head fuck.

E-J: My arm is too thin for phallosplasty. They can't get the fat off there, so the only place would be my tummy, but off my tummy you would have zero sensation because there is no nerve reconnection there, so for me it would mean looking down and seeing my stomach hanging down between my legs with no function. That's never going to meet my cock expectations.

At the moment I can still wank and I can still come and spurt, and I do, often. I love coming. I'm not willing to give that up for a false expectation that surgery would be the answer. That is not going to work for me for a number of different reasons. But as a consequence, I can't displace not having a phallus, because that's where my dysphoria lies. I have to pack every day. I sleep with my packer. I have to feel like there is weight and shape there. Internally it settles my soul. A term that almost rings true to me is like having a 'ghost limb'. I feel like something's not right physically and I can't even go without packing. That real physical disembodiment is the seed of my dysphoria. So, regardless of how I can enjoy my physicality and come to terms with my expectations that surgery's not going to work, about every three months I have big sobbing sessions, a huge cry and go, 'I have to have surgery, I don't know what else I'm going to fucking do', and panic and panic and panic. I have two weeks of really, really heavy sadness, and then I slowly get out of it again. I wank myself out of it and then I say to myself, 'You have to come to terms with it. That's life. You can't waste your whole time worrying about it.'

I feel like I have arrived at a happy medium, maybe by confronting the physical impacts and effects of surgery (like the erectile tissue left behind, which at first repulsed me as it represented maleness but is a centre of pleasure now). It allowed me to find a way to be at one and at peace with my altered body. But I needed to leave the concept of gendered spaces behind. I used to ignore my arse because of the soft downy hair around my hole – again, because I defined that stupidly as male. In many ways, allowing my transness to exist as my sole identity allowed me to connect with my fractured body and allow it to knit. I can make sense of the bits that look real and the bits that have sensation and innate pleasure. I wonder if we took charge much more of our processes?

E-J: My problem still is that if and when I look down I see woman. I have techniques of wanking that make me feel more masculine, but at the end of the day it is that visual disconnect. I feel like I have lived with this for so long that I know this is where I am at. I can't get to that celebration space.

It happened under my old olive tree. Maybe it's a magical space – come out and see if it works for you.

E-J: I'd love to. My sanity lies in loving my queerness. I find my transness hard but my queerness I wouldn't change anything about. I fucking love it. It makes me want to dance down the street. I look at other people who aren't queer and feel how lucky I am to have this 360 experience of life. My world is colourful, open-minded and creative. The people in my life are so complex and extraordinary and challenging. That for me is my pleasure zone – my queerness – but my transness for me is my body, and my body is private and that for me is a place of pain. I queer it and it is that queerness that allows me to have access and fun.

In your work, the Museum of Transology, your curation, you understand artifice and the object and its collective and individual meaning in our world. I often think that trans freedom, on many levels, relies on the world being able to reinterpret genitals away from gender, i.e. a vagina can be male and a cock can be female. Do you think that is possible, perhaps outside of your own experience?

E-J: I have a much bigger clitoris. I wank and embrace my bigger clit as a form of masculinity, and that feels like progress. I try and do different sexual moves than I see outside of porn. Language really helps. Using masculine language for my genitalia helps me place it in a different space. I think that our ideas of normativity and functionality with our genitalia is an imagined version anyway, because we all know men have problems with their cocks and how they work, we all know that people have problems and issues with all of their bodies, and so I think this uber-aspiration and drive for a perfect body is a trans pressure that we place on ourselves. That is misinformed.

I think our desire for a perfect set of genitals, perfectly working, perfectly received and perfectly encountered is punishing and often fanciful.

E-J: Look at sales of Viagra. Cocks don't stay hard, they go soft, they dribble. But we are not immune to the notion of the perfect body. You only have to go back to what Naomi Wolf says about this. This wisdom has been there in the feminist world for so long. It is another form of patriarchal oppression that drives this idea that it is possible to achieve this perfect, all-round stud-like erectile prowess that is not realistic. It's linked not only to our experience of being trans but it's linked to the broader oppression of body normativity and body beautiful that our community is doubly susceptible to because we are taught to feel so bad about ourselves, and we're taught that we are so different, and we're taught that we are not allowed to have power to shape who we are and who we want to be. In order to embrace that power we already feel like we are in a fight rather than in a moment of glory and growth. One day people will be able to go and chop their cocks off like having a haircut, just like having lip fillers or a facelift. We are just in a mis-place in history in which the world hasn't caught up with where we want to go.

Where everyone wants to go with gender.

E-J: Everyone. This is not just a trans experience. This is linked to the broader oppression of all bodies, linked to the commodification, the commercialisation and the beautification of our bodies. This is part of the larger blanket that we all live under, us included – trans people cannot magically live apart from this.

We are taught that to make our bodies be as we want we are in a fight, a struggle, instead of going, 'This is proactive, this is something to be celebrated, this is empowerment, this is a living example of someone who is self-aware and empowered.'

Instead, in the negative framework we are placed as readjusting and aspiring to 'their perfection'. It's all the wrong way round.

The conversation starts off with us as being broken and not the system, the system presented as woke and us needing training and learning. We would repair for them and to them, we would look real for them.

E-J: I think that there is another thing that we haven't spoken about yet and that is the medical system itself; that, in actual fact, the majority of people working in the system are cis men, and the ideal that they aspire to achieve for us is through their lens as is the whole medical system. So you are walking into a room that is already in a framework of repair that is according to that normative standard and you have very little power to reframe that. There are so few doctors, full stop, who do phallosplasty. Compare that to the numbers of doctors who work on trans women, and why is that? Well, men don't want to build the perfect cock; it's a threat to masculinity anyway. What if it can be constructed? They are willing to imagine the perfect vagina they can construct but much less willing to imagine the perfect cock.

But even their idea of a perfect vagina is often looking real and depth. I suspect with more one-on-one time there might be more scope to talk pleasure, but still it's limited because of binary thinking. The depth is often used as their mark of success, thus depth taken a day or so after the packing has come out.

E-J: I'm surprised they don't give it a go. It's constructed through the male surgical gaze and they are coming up with the solutions.

In my field – I work in heritage and museums – we will never halt the erasure or overlooking of trans history without having trans people within the heritage sector looking at and recognising the stories and reframing them. In the same way, how can we have the surgical solutions that really fit the possibilities of what our bodies can become unless we have trans people being our surgeons? It's a huge process of change we are talking about, so coming back to the question of whether trans people can change the world: yes, they fucking can. Imagine if trans people were the surgeons, the historians. This would be more than them finding trans solutions, this would be about dismantling dysfunctional systems on every level.

I feel blown away talking to you. For me this all starts with me just using the word 'trans'. It starts to try and set up our own space, structures, away from the dysfunction of gender. I used 'femme' for a time, 'trans femme', but it made no sense to keep attaching myself to a space that I massively disagreed with. It was still patriarchy. That's why I find 'nonbinary' tough, even though in terms of gender it feels like a space that is creating space; but, for me, its attachment to 'binary' is problematic especially when we can use 'trans' and make it as vast as we want. 'Trans' challenges for me in a way that 'nonbinary' doesn't.

E-J: I wanted to talk about that. I'm a stickler for words because I'm a writer and I find it problematic – not conceptually, but because I don't want to see people starting off naming their identity with a negative. To be 'non' is to be incomplete, and also by saying 'nonbinary' you reinforce the 'binary'. I would argue that there is a spectrum that is circular and not linear with two ends. I think it is a circular thing that moves and has cogs, like a clock, that move. So, for me, to say that you are 'nonbinary' is to first say there is a 'binary' and you are not part of it, you are the incomplete (in relation to language). I love 'genderqueer' because it's about queering the process, an eruption and celebration and a rejection of 'their' language.

I just don't want to be in opposition my whole life. I want to find a resting space and a comfortable space that is trans and queer, both for me and my genitals. At a push, I'd ask people to use 'they'/'them' pronouns, but I'd rather my name be used. 'Trans' and 'queer' have space, vast undiscovered space. We have been taught to reject being queer and pass through trans as speedily as possible to enter the binary. That doesn't work on any level for me. I can't be oppositional to binaries, because they are bust and I aim to operate on a deeper level.

If you could envisage a future in which trans folk had a completely equal stake on this planet and an ownership of our identities, a trans world, what might it look like? What might surgery look like?

E-J: [*Long pause.*] I think there is a lot of potential to be more creative and to use a combination of what we have and what we want, rather than one or the other: a blend. For me, that surgery would displace what doesn't feel right for me, without aspiring to be the unachievable. I use the pronoun 'he' because it's been an incredibly long journey to become the kind of man I wanted to be, and I am a version of he that disrupts what he normally is, and to show what he can be. I'd never feel ashamed of using or being 'he', but it does feel like part of the problem of enforcing binaries.

I think it's entirely valid to occupy the pronoun you feel works for you, especially when you are challenging that pronoun to be more, to be different. 'She'/'her' never allowed me that space in a way that 'they'/'them' does. The performance of 'she' took over, but my genitals are definitely 'queer' and I had to shift to match them.*

E-J: Trans potential is always going to be aligned with my queerness. It's always the celebration of my queerness, the unknown and the direction I/we can take that in. When we trust the unknown that's exciting. Every smile of my day is in the Venn diagram in between trans and queer.

I worry that our creativity, the creativity of trans, isn't being realised yet. It's become a very linear fight.

E-J: Yes, our otherness needs to be celebrated as it challenges everything.

We are the future, aren't we?

E-J: Yes, we are.

* * *

Following our interview, I have to admit that I'm incredibly attracted to E-J, not in a heavy-handed, romantic or sexual way, but attracted to him as a person, as someone I think I want to hang out with. He shines. He truly shines.

His home is one of the most comfortable, comforting and welcoming spaces that I have been in for years, and his smile radiates out gloriously.

He is like a 'genderqueer sage', a twinkling, rather beautiful genderqueer sage.

I could have watched him and listened to him talk all day. When he talks, movements ripple from his hands to his feet and then across his facial features. Animated and serious.

E-J feels like one of the most alive people I have ever encountered, his energy fizzes and sparkles. It would be hard to not fall for E-J's charms because I'm absolutely sure he's not overly aware of them. He is both humble and poetically intelligent. There's also a nervousness which I'm pretty sure must fuel his search for comfort, for the right words and for safety. I recognise that nervousness. I often feed off the same nervous energy, but mine is finite, whereas E-J's feels boundless. There's also a slight tinge, a seam, of heavy sadness.

A genitalia sadness.

The word 'trans' makes E-J feel dysphoric. I have never considered that before, because for me the word is affirming. 'Trans' is my saviour, my saving grace. But for E-J it is problematic as it raises all notions of genitals: his genitals as they are, as they might possibly be and the potential challenges E-J sees in the surgical cock-creation processes for trans masculine folk. It made me stop and think about my connection to the word 'trans' and why it is that I can accept a trans solution to my genitals and be utterly content with them not being a simple binary outcome – a vagina; rather, I see them as trans-genitals which mix and blend the actual with the performative and the philosophical and perhaps even the political. I only judge my genitals against my genitals, against my enjoyment of them and my experience of them. E-J sits the other side of 'perfect cock', feeling imperfect.

The word 'trans' to me is different to the word that E-J perceives it to be, maybe because in very binary terms the surgery for trans women and trans femmes is far more straight-forward and perhaps more successful than for trans men and trans masculine peeps. I haven't seen or experienced enough trans cocks to say that with any certainty. Many of the people I have interviewed are incredibly happy with their version of cock, but there does seem to be a difference in the simplicity of the surgical process.

The medical profession have perfected the look of a trans vagina. As we live within a sexist framework where men are really terrified of vaginas, no one is going to look that closely, and who cares if we experience pleasure anyway when at least we look the part?

E-J talked about the misogyny endemic within the field of trans realignment surgery and within healthcare more widely. This is something I have often felt from a femme perspective, based on my experience of the lack of male surgical attention paid to pleasure when creating a neo-vagina. Talking with E-J allowed me some space to consider if or why the surgical attention paid to trans women is or might be far greater than that paid to trans men where there is still obviously so much more work to be done to perfect the process and to get us all to a level surgical playing field.

Genitals are as much about play as they are about merely looking the part, and play for a cock means to be able to become erect and to piss standing up. Most of the vulvic actions are, for the best part, hidden or experienced intimately – no shared urinals and no erections needed.

As surgically crafted genitals go, neo-vulvas exist and work on many of those levels. They, more than often, look the part. They structurally have all the right bits in all the right places: clitoris, vagina, urethral opening, labia and vulvic proximity to everything else. The neo-vagina sits near to your arse in exactly the same place as it would on any woman, and all of the bits in the right places appear to work properly. This is vastly simplistic, I know, but generically, trans vaginas are pretty much a done-deal product within the confines of our sexist parameters. The methodology between paid-for and free healthcare vaginoplasty is pretty similar, if not exactly the same, practised the same for almost a hundred years.

To be able to feel and get better pleasure, we need to challenge the patriarchal mindset that deems that our female depth is more important than our pleasure. But pleasure aside, neo-vaginas are a design that in principle works, time and time again, like the Kenwood Chef.

But – and this is feedback from friends and people I have interviewed – the surgery for trans men isn't anywhere near that straightforward if we are to use the very basic marker of the fictional standard porn cock, which in our patriarchal society is depicted as heavy and hanging when flaccid and bigger and hard when erect, with both cock states sitting atop a big pair of evenly sized balls (golf ball size). This standard cock is and has always been fictionalised as being perfect in shape, size and workability.

As a person with a history of sex work, principally servicing cis male clients, I can attest to that being an absolute load of bullshit.

Cocks are infinitely different in every way but are just presented and therefore perceived idealistically by (cis) male society as being the very pinnacle of masculine prowess and power: the thrusting, ever-ready, ever-spunking cock, pushing, shoving, shooting.

The cock is never presented as the fragile or humble member that is too shy to peek out: the reticent cock, the timid cock, the exploratory cock. If a cock is ever deemed to be less than powerful, it is often presented as the cuckold cock, the tiny cock, the useless cock. So harsh are these judgements that men create for men.

One of the things I had to learn very quickly as a sex worker was how to talk men down from their perceived failure to get an erection, to come, or to powerfully and visibly ejaculate. Often their fear of failure sat dangerously close to their rising anger caused by their deeply felt embarrassment – visceral embarrassment which is completely cock-based. We might joke, but cock stuff can really break a man. I've known men to cry.

It's a fine art trying to make someone come when they can't but really want to and need to, and then to nurse their ego, all for a few quid or drugs; but it felt like one of the decent things I could do in the job.

It all comes back to the idea that society holds and perpetuates about the cock as an icon, being godlike, powerful and certain. Cocks are painted as definite. Across many cultures power was often depicted by a male figure – a big, small or indifferent male figure – fronted by a massive, out-of-proportion phallus. It was seen as the perfect symbol for power.

As a sex worker, I remember many men wanting to experience touch and caresses on or around their genitals but being terrified of revealing their cock. The confident punter was much rarer than you'd think.

Penises are so power-complex, whilst vulvas are almost completely ignored. Every man thinks he knows his way around a vulva, so making one that looks real must seem an easy task to men who have the power of surgical ability. Vulvas and vaginas are not seen as powerful spaces. A cock's ability, its power play, relies on its inherent and natural ability to get erect. When you are trying to craft that power play through gender realignment surgery, you are trying to craft an act, a movement and not a static being.

Considering the symbolic power given to penises within our society/societies, you would have thought that there would be much more of a concerted effort put into the surgical creation of them by men keen to keep the 'dick energy strong'. Yet it also makes perfect sense in a patriarchal society that men would be far more invested in creating the 'perfect pussy' as it's a space they can imagine fucking without really needing to understand or care about the woman's pleasure; but to create a dick from scratch might slightly undo the notion of the totemic natural beast of a cock. A trans neo-vagina is a static inwards looking organ that the surgeons know they can do. In a simplistic *quid pro quo* way it's a good day at the office. Trans neo-cocks must also provide that but in a much less certain and much more expensive way. Surgeons, from my experience, like to be right, like to sign off from a good day at the office. It makes sense.

I do not know enough about the technical side of cock creation for trans men – its successes or its downsides – to make any definitive statements, but what I do know has been gathered by listening to trans and nonbinary masculine friends speak about the lack of clarity and certainty inherent in the process. I did feel certainty (there weren't many, if any, unknowns) in the trans neo-vagina process. For trans men and trans masculine folk there still feels like there is an element of stepping off into the unknown, whereas we trans women follow a well-trodden path – the surgical process is in great detail on YouTube, our healing follows very similar paths and timeframes, and the only things that might not work (our pleasure, for example) are invisible to the eye.

We really must support our trans brothers and masculine siblings in their fight for surgical parity. I feel like an incredibly bad ally as I have no idea of the funding available, the ease of getting funded, the waiting lists and the hoops that my trans masculine siblings have to jump through to get the surgery they need.

The trans men I have met, and am lucky enough to know and count as friends, often exemplify a form of detoxified masculinity and an almost contemporary version of masculinity that invests wonderfully in the nuances of masculinity whilst expanding it to contain so, so much more: for starters, feminism, which comes from a lived experience. Can men be feminists? Yes, trans men get it, they really get it. We just need to give them the space to talk about it. I suspect deep down it's our historical male privilege that allows us to jump into feminism without consulting them first.

That's such a massive sea change that we seldom thank trans masculine peeps for. The idea that a man or a someone trans who defines themselves as masculine can truly understand why feminism exists from a lived perspective is huge in terms of changing and challenging the structures of patriarchy. Trans men and trans masculine people hold so many of the keys.

Words and labels are incredibly important – vital – but they should breathe life into us and not suck it out, they should allow light in and not shut it out, they should allow a soul to dance and not a soul to die. My word, my label, 'trans', allows me to breathe but forces E-J to confront a cycle of dysphoria.

E-J allowed me to think deeply about that, about the word that gives me life.

I adored everything about meeting E-J: their soul, their vulnerability and the journey they took me on with their story and their fine ability to curate our time together.

TRANS IS BEAUTIFUL

I read a piece recently: one of those trans horror-story pieces that starts in the *Daily Mail* and ends up as a debate with Piers Morgan on *Good Morning Britain* or perhaps Nick Ferrari on LBC, and that has all the 'apparent' right-thinking people throwing their hands in the air and claiming that the world has gone mad: '*Whatever next, a man who feels he is really an elephant?*' Trans debates reduced to the absurd for white cis men and women to toss between them in their sanctified game of illusory self-righteousness.

Tossers.

The story was about a school with seventeen pupils who, to paraphrase, are 'changing genders'. There is a bubbling expectation of public outrage all around the story. Piers is frothing and his Catholic guest is horrified, sat next to the single trans adult rolled out to represent all of transdom to try and inject some sanity into the hysteria, what we really know is that they are simply part and parcel of the now common, 'bash the mentally ill trans brigade' routine that ends with a man like Piers saying, '*Tomorrow, dear viewers, I will be coming in as a grasshopper*'.

The world at large imagines accidently treading on a large, whiny grasshopper.

My thoughts on hearing the story were thank fuck. The story was in reality about a comparatively *small* group of children in a *large* school, questioning their assigned genders.

'Thank fuck,' I thought.

Thank fuck that we are finally beginning to realise that we control and own gender rather than it controlling and owning us. If gender has a place, its place is to please us, and it's not for us to be spending our lives trying to please or placate it. Without us acting or performing gender, it is inert and meaningless.

I thought thank fuck that we, or more specifically the younger trans we, are taking gender by the scruff and refusing to be enthralled and captured by it in a submissive lifelong struggle to fit into its prescriptive and punishing remit. The performance of gender, be it cis or trans, is always punishing. We always lose and we only ever get to stand still in fragility, having the appearance of standing still.

The story felt like a day to celebrate, and celebrate we must because the train has already left the station and it's not going back in the shed. We're not going back in the shed or the closet.

The change is happening and we've arrived at this miraculous point a few short years after the apparent trans tipping point. There is of course a horrible kickback, a spiteful and often violent kickback, a set of people determined for the world to remain exactly as they see fit because the narrowness of the bandwidth works for them: a white cis male and some white cis female bandwidth.

But they are the very same people who were against LGB liberation and equality. I know, I lived through it, and back in the late 80s and early 90s I was part of one of the first LGBT housing cooperatives set up in London to offer security to the many young lesbian, gay or trans folk who had been kicked out of their family homes or rented homes when their sexuality had come to light. We had to hide back then most of the time. We had to be careful about our houses and their locations for fear of homophobic, lesphobic or transphobic attacks.

I recognise the same people speaking out now against our right to equality and against younger trans folk coming to their sense of authenticity at an earlier point in their lives rather than wasting year after painful year being hidden under layer upon layer of shame and fear. It is the very same people, although now they try to hide their pernicious aims by saying that they understand gay and lesbian issues but not 'this gender stuff'. Divide the minorities and get them to fight each other: butch lesbians and trans men, and femme gay men and trans women.

The gender binary doesn't even really work for those people attacking us now from their binary perches. They seek to use gender to harm others and control others. If the gender binary worked so well for them, they wouldn't be attacking us as they'd feel safe and secure, nestled in the arms of the gender binary.

The brave, wonderful young people in schools up and down the country, questioning their gender and making it fit them, are doing the work of usualising trans identities so that the generations that come after them and us will be able to enter school knowing that *'becoming the best that they can be'* includes 'becoming the best of gender that they choose to be'. This is an emerging generation who know that genitals just equal genitals, that they do not sum up gender or frame gender and that they can be altered or reconfigured to fit more comfortably. Supporting them is a joyous thing. They are life, they are future.

It's jarring to see some trans folk – mainly older white trans women (just a tiny minority) – collaborating with our opponents and saying some pretty awful stuff about 'the trans lobby indoctrinating children and ruining their lives with puberty blockers and cross sex hormones', as if they were available at the tuck shop along with the other penny chews. It's strange to see a small group of mainly older white trans women demand that we don't shift gender whilst at the same time saying, with some older white cis feminists, that gender needs shifting in order to free up women and girls from the yoke of gender expectation. Somehow they never countenance the idea that it might need a joint effort from us all, trans people included, to shift and gently smash the patriarchal gender roles that have dogged our world for so long. For some reason, that small group of mainly older white trans and cis men and women, assume that gender in young trans hands is a dangerous, omnipotent power that can never be trusted.

Young trans folk are not to be trusted to make gender decisions about themselves – decisions they make naturally, day in day out, by just asking the world to see and encounter them as they feel they truly are. As they feel comfortable.

Rather, that small group of mainly white older trans and cis folk would like us to continue to be funnelled through a difficult, medicalised, pathological pathway in which we are allowed access to gender through the controlled gateway of lofty 'paternalistic gender care'. As trans folk we have been drip-fed gender through the cis idea of what their gender means to them. That's why, after surgery, my surgeon was keen to push a speculum deep inside of me, as far as it could go, and tell me my depth without my ever asking him for this information. I was made woman by his idea of a woman. Younger trans folk will change this if we allow and support them, because they will ask for more (and ironically they may ask for less): different surgeries, different pathways, different outcomes.

Of course for many of us, me included, our genital configurations need to be changed to fit us more precisely and comfortably, but the word 'woman' that came along with my neo-vulvic configuration didn't make any more sense to me than the word 'man'. I was assigned male at birth and then reassigned, shoehorned, into another gender performance model through the overly simplistic medical process. Cock equals men and vulva equals woman. As trans folk, we have to challenge the patriarchy and the gender binary in order to exist happy and true. It doesn't mean that we can't be women or men if that makes us feel comfortable, or nonbinary or fluid if those work for us, but we cannot be submissive to patriarchy and the gender binary and expect to find comfort within it. It is an uncomfortable space even for those who never have to question it. Claiming trans as a destination turns the whole process on its head and asks more questions about what kind of empowered space(s) we want to evolve into. We really are the single group in society to really see gender from a much broader perspective as long as we are prepared to let go, even a little, of gender itself.

I am not placing fault with the medical structures that support gender realignment, because they exist within the same patriarchal and sexist confines and context. But one of the most common things I hear now is genderqueer, nonbinary and gender fluid people worrying if the current system of gender therapy and realignment will take them seriously and listen to them if they don't want to take a binary pathway: if they don't have an A and a B in their lives.

There's real fear that they will either not be taken seriously, or that they will have to adapt their desires to fit a binary pathway. This doesn't mean the system is broken, rather that the system needs to be reviewed alongside our contemporary notions of womanhood, feminism, masculinity and toxicity. Gender realignment or reassignment cannot exist in a vacuum outside of feminism or political meaning or exist outside of the changing face and role of gender within society. Some people will want more and some will want or need less. We have to allow for shades of grey, and rather than just asking if people feel like a woman or feel like a man, let's encourage people to describe how they feel, then hear them and trust them.

If I could have done, I would have taken blockers at twelve because I knew deep down that the feelings rising up at puberty were confirming a maleness that made me feel acutely uncomfortable and at odds with the world. I felt outside of my body. Deep down my soul was never male. I would have taken blockers and I would always have had my trans-affirming surgery, only, for me, I wish it could have been seen and spoken of as trans-affirming rather than binary-affirming, which never made sense. Trans provides this kind of critically creative framework for this exploration and denunciation of the most harmful aspects of gender. When I look down at my genitals, or lie with my legs open and study them in a mirror, I don't perceive male or female. I experience and feel them as being only trans. For me there is a third way but it isn't a third gender, it is simply a movement away from gender to a grey space that isn't about confirmation. My genitals certainly don't need a gender reveal party.

Gender should feel like a gift to grow into at our own pace, with reconfiguration if desired.

I adore Travis's theory that we are all trans, meaning that if we remove the enforcement of gender at birth, via the route of simple genital recognition, then we can all decide how best to live out this life of ours. We can grow into being us rather than grow into someone's idea of us. This isn't a minority trying to enforce their ideas onto the majority but it is a minority saying that gender doesn't really work for anybody, not in this way, not in the way we are held prisoners to gender, like Stockholm captives en-masse born into gender slavery, on both sides. Look at the suicide rates for young cis men trying to be young cis men. The gender binary is a broken, harmful construct being kept alive by a few people who feel without it they won't exist and a few people for whom it works day in and day out by allowing them unfettered access to power and privilege.

It makes sense to many people to hold on by their finger tips to the gender binary. It's a short life and the gender binary gives them the illusion, from a distance, of comfort (even if a single person's comfort makes a thousand others feel uncomfortable). But up close and personal the gender binary is nothing but pain, sometimes the slow silent drip of pain – a million images of the way you're told you should look (or sometimes the brutalising pain of misogyny, directed violently towards women) that the binary deems need to be kept in check, by the binary itself.

I know this is a plea in the dark, but to those in my community speaking out against young trans folk finding their sense of gender, I say, 'Please, rather than demonise them, let's support them because they are brick by brick taking down the structures that hold all of us in the grip of a binary system that exists, not giving a shit if we are happy or sad.'

I ask those few trans women who speak out demanding that we leave gender just the way it is because although it needs smashing it can't possibly be us who are trusted to smash it, to consider that it is really years of male privilege speaking out rather than any sense of newly grown feminism. Why deny others that which you now hold dear?

The empowerment and autonomy we see in young trans folk who wish to express their gender any way they choose is testament to the loosening of gender demands and expectations that we have all collaborated to change over these past years. Perhaps we all need to calm down and recognise that young people questioning their gender is the perfect outcome to feminism, first, second or third wave, and not something that has just popped up as a contagious fashion statement to oppose and demolish women's rights.

Let's not pitch that fight.

Young gender questioning people are the logical and necessary outcome of our desire to break the stranglehold of gender that negatively impacts all of our lives. We are winning the battle and maybe even the war, and it is being led, on all fronts, by the very young feeling that they have the right to live a life on their own terms. Kate Bornstein was the elder whose voice offered me hope and a space to exist in with dignity and comfort. It is only right as I become an elder in our community that I redouble my efforts to ensure that we support our young trans people by speaking my truth, however vulnerable that truth might make me feel.

Using the word 'trans' alone without qualification does that, It stands up proud, it's radical and bold in the face of attack and in the face of gender demands. It provides a comfortable space for others to grow up in without needing any words – perhaps future lives without labels. 'Trans' alone is a finger up to gender expectations and limitations.

The word 'trans', as a destination, has the capacity to truly shake the patriarchal structures to the ground. Patriarchy cannot cope with us occupying our own trans bodies and trans identities. We unsettle and force colossal rethinks about gender, gender expectations and gender stereotypes when we introduce the new idea that our transness alone is the aim. The words 'passing' and 'blending' are owned by the binary, not us, never us.

Trans as a destination is aspirational.

To amplify our transness, as opposed to diminishing it and dampening it down through the simple adoption of gender normativity, cis normativity and heteronormativity, is to find vast amounts of new space in a world which only ever gives the illusion of space.

Transness really is new space. Transness is uncontrolled and uncontrollable by patriarchy.

If I'm to describe my genitals, I will do so by stating their spacious truth: a cunt made from a cock, an orifice lined with cock and ball skin, which defies labelling and demands that a new space opens up in this world of ours.

Trans-genitals.

Maybe it will not become safe and comfortable for all in my lifetime, but the ripple in the Bornstein pond has started and it cannot be stopped. This is a short life that we live and we owe ourselves comfort in this life, joy in this life and the chance to experience love in this life. We can only do this if we are living our authentic truth and not if we are being forced to hide in a gendered body that makes others smile at our expense.

At the end of my last book I said that I desperately wanted a cuddle and a kiss but at the end of this book I am happy to report that under my old olive tree I experience pleasure in my trans body like I never have experienced pleasure before: pleasure that comes from being utterly present in every fibre, sinew and cell of my body; thankful for every curve, mound, stitch mark, reconfigured orifice, every hair and every line on my face that defines me as being alive in my own sense of self.

I feel only trans, nothing more. I need nothing more, simply I am Trans-sapiens.

Georgia O'Keeffe said that she yearned for *'big wide open skies and to be able to be happy by herself in a landscape as vast as an ocean'*. Trans to me is that ocean, that landscape, that sky. Trans is beautiful.